The Contented Child's Food Bible

The Contented Child's Food Bible

The complete guide to feeding 0–6-year olds

Gina Ford and Paul Sacher

Vermilion
LONDON

First published in the United Kingdom in 2004
by Vermilion, an imprint of Ebury Press
Random House UK Ltd
Random House
20 Vauxhall Bridge Road
London SW1V 2SA

www.randomhouse.co.uk

Addresses for companies within
The Random House Group Limited can be found at:
www.randomhouse.co.uk/offices.htm

Random House UK Limited Reg. No. 954009

A CIP catalogue record for this book is available from the British Library

ISBN: 9780091891565

Penguin Random House is committed to a sustainable future for our business, our readers and our planet. This book is made from Forest Stewardship Council® certified paper.

Printed and bound in Great Britain by Clays Ltd, St Ives plc

Please note that conversions to imperial weights and measures are suitable equivalents and not exact.

The information given in this book should not be treated as a substitute for qualified medical advice; always consult a medical practitioner. Neither the authors nor the publisher can be held responsible for any loss or claim arising out of the use, or misuse, of the suggestions made or the failure to take medical advice.

The information and advice contained within this book is not necessarily representative of the views of Great Ormond Street Hospital for Children NHS Trust. The Hospital cannot accept any legal responsibility for any injury, illness or harm sustained as a result of following recommendations in this book.

Acknowledgements

A huge thank you to my family and friends who have continued to give me their unconditional love and support. Special love and thanks to darling Molly who continues to be the best CLB boxer, ever. A very special thank you to my agent Emma Todd whose insight into parenting and publishing, and enormous support and encouragement has given me the strength to persevere with my writing. Thank you to Paul Sacher, my co-author for doing such a brilliant job of explaining all aspects of the nutritional needs of young children. It has been inspirational to work with a professional who cares so passionately about the health of young children and understands the importance of presenting parents with the information they need in such a clear, simple and concise way. Finally, a special thank you to those parents who have worked with me during the writing of this book, without your continued feed back and belief in my advice, the case studies in this book would not have been possible. Thank you to Fiona MacIntyre for recognising the value of our work and to Lesley McOwan, Dawn Fozard and all the team at Random House.

Gina Ford

Thank you to my parents, Clive and Annette. Thank you, David, for all your encouragement and support, even when things were a mystery. Mandy and Ivan for their love and support. The Sher family for always being there for me in good and bad times. My friend and agent, Chris Calitz, for all his words of wisdom and guidance. To Vanessa Shaw, for proofreading the text. To Lesley McOwan for masterminding this book and Dawn Fozard for pulling it all together. Last but not least, a final thanks to all my colleagues at Great Ormond Street Hospital and all the patients I have seen over the last eight years for providing with me with constant inspiration and material for this book.

Paul Sacher

Contents

Introduction

We both firmly believe that feeding should not be a cause of anxiety for either children or parents and that common eating concerns can be solved with practical and simple advice. We have been able to combine our experience and knowledge to write *The Contented Child's Food Bible* with the aim of guiding parents through the problems, questions and challenges posed to them during a baby's and child's early years. In this book we:

- aim to help parents avoid many of the pitfalls that often confront them, and reassure them when they are presented with eating issues relating to their child.

- address a child's nutritional needs stage by stage and offer comprehensive advice to deal with the challenges presented from weaning to six years old. With levels of obesity rising in the young, and myriad advice in newspapers and magazines, it is difficult to know what guidelines to apply to your own child. His eating habits are formed from observing those around him. He will also be affected by what he observes on television. The children's food business is a multi-million pound industry which promotes many foods high in fat, sugar and salt. There is now clear evidence linking a child's nutrition with his intellectual and physical development in later life.

- offer the most up-to-date nutritional information. All children are different. We hope to find solutions for the most common parental worries, such as encouraging children to eat more fruit and vegetables, to more significant concerns including when a child eats very little of good nutritional content at all. We feel that with the right approach and emphasis every child can learn good eating habits, which not only will make them happy and healthy, but which also give them a good relationship with food that will last a lifetime.

The advice throughout applies to healthy children only. It is not for those who may have digestive disorders or medical conditions that affect their eating. Neither does it apply to children who have emotional or behavioural problems which often require medical supervision and even psychological intervention. This book is not intended to replace medical advice and if, at any time, you are concerned about your child's health please seek advice from a qualified medical or health professional (see page 201).

Gina Ford and Paul Sacher

1
Healthy Food for Growing Children

Good nutrition is all about balance – ensuring that your child gets all the essential nutrients from a variety of foods. To help you achieve this balance you need to become familiar with the four main food groups, each of which comprises foods that provide similar nutrients. For example, all the foods in Group One are dairy products, which supply energy, protein and good levels of calcium.

Try to visualise the groups when you are preparing meals for your child, as choosing at least one food from each group will help you to achieve dietary balance. For example, meatballs (Group Four) with mashed potato containing butter and milk (Groups One and Two) and peas (Group Three) is a well-balanced meal. Serving your child from the four main food groups goes a long way towards ensuring that he receives the right balance of essential nutrients.

Food Groups

Group One: milk and dairy products
Breast milk, infant formula, cow's milk, lassi, yoghurt, fromage frais, cottage cheese and hard cheese.

Major nutrients
Energy (calories) from lactose and fat; protein, calcium, vitamins A and B, zinc; iron and vitamin D (only in breast and formula milks).

6–7 months
Minimum of 600ml (20oz) daily of breast milk or formula, inclusive of milk used in solids, such as yoghurt. You can introduce full-fat natural yoghurt, unsweetened fromage frais and cheese sauce. If your baby is between four months and six months old and appears still to be hungry please speak to your Health Visitor about the best course of action.

7–9 months
Minimum of 500–600ml (17–20oz) daily of breast, formula or follow-on milk, inclusive of milks used in solids. Hard cheese can be used in sauces, and cubed or grated as a finger food. Cow's milk can be used on cereals and in cooking, but if your child is not getting the minimum quantity of breast or formula milk, use it on cereals and in cooking. You can give him full-fat, smooth-style yoghurts and fromage frais. Also try dairy desserts, such as milk puddings and fruit mousses with no added sugar.

9–12 months
Minimum of 500–600ml (17–20oz) daily of breast milk, formula milk or follow-on milk, inclusive of milk used in solids. Full-fat yoghurts and fromage frais with fruit pieces can also be given.

1–6 years
Sufficient milk after one year is important to ensure your child gets enough calcium for strong bones. The daily recommendation is 500ml (17oz) (minimum amount 350ml/12oz) for 1–2 year olds and 350ml (12oz) for children over two years old, but this does not have to be drunk as milk, and can include other dairy products. For example, one pot of yoghurt 125g (4½oz) or 30g (1oz) of cheese can be substituted for 210ml (7oz) of milk. So if, during a day, your five-year-old child has 210ml (7oz) of milk with his breakfast cereal or as a drink, then has a pot of yoghurt, he will be meeting the recommendation. Aim to give dairy products at least three times a day.

Gina Ford's Top Tip

If your toddler loses interest in his breakfast cereal, try mixing it with yoghurt instead of milk.

Q **My child won't drink plain milk; what should I do?**

A Milk can be used in drinks, such as milkshakes, with breakfast cereals and in puddings and sauces. To keep up your child's intake of calcium, offer cheese as a snack and include some cheese triangles with packed lunches. Sprinkle grated cheese on meals and vegetables, and serve dishes such as macaroni cheese or cauliflower cheese. Yoghurts and fromage frais are good sources of calcium and come in many different flavours. Do not use low-fat varieties because children need fat to grow well, and the low-fat ones also tend to be packed with sugar or artificial sweeteners. For calcium contents of some common foods (see page 37).

Understanding milk

Many common nutritional problems are caused by children having too little, too much, or the wrong type of milk, so make sure your child doesn't fall into this trap. Babies who don't get enough milk will grow poorly because they won't be meeting their full nutritional requirements of energy, protein, vitamins and minerals. On the other hand, babies who are overfed might gain excessive weight, which could lead to being overweight when they are older. Use the table overleaf to make sure your child is getting the most appropriate milk for his age.

Advice on weaning from milk

Once breast-feeding is established, continue for as long as possible up to one year of age, but at least until 4–6 months, when solids are introduced. The 2003 Department of Health (DoH)

Milk requirements for children

Age	Type of milk
0–6 months	Breast milk or infant formula (from birth or first stage).
6 months–1 year	As above, plus follow-on formulas (6 months–2 years).
1–2 years	Full-fat cow's milk or follow-on formula.
2–5 years	Semi-skimmed cow's milk (also known as low-fat milk) may be used. If you are concerned about poor growth, stick to full-fat milk.
5 years onwards	Semi-skimmed cow's milk. Skimmed cow's milk (also known as fat-free milk) may be used if your child is growing well.

guidelines were prompted by World Health Organisation recommendations that advise breast-feeding exclusively for the first six months of life, i.e. no solids or infant formulas. Babies receiving breast-milk substitutes (infant formulas) should also have weaning onto solids delayed until six months. However, previous advice was to wean between four and six months, and mothers might wish to start solids before six months. Solids should not be given before four months (17 weeks), whether babies are breast-fed or bottle-fed. As all babies are different, it is important to watch for signs that your baby is ready to start weaning (see page 86).

Remember that the DoH advice is a guideline and that not all babies will be ready to do things at the same time. Judge your baby's individual needs.

- If you are breast-feeding your baby or giving infant formula or a mixture of both, you can continue to do so without introducing solids for six months, provided your baby is not showing signs of being too hungry.

- If you feel your baby is ready for solids earlier than six months, do not be tempted to give them before four months (17 weeks).

Q Which is best – cow's milk or follow-on formula?

A Cow's milk can replace breast milk and formula milk after
12 months, but it is important to remember that cow's milk
is not a good source of iron. Some babies are poor eaters
and may be very fussy, refusing to eat foods containing
iron. In these cases, follow-on formulas may be a solution,
as they contain added vitamins and minerals, including
iron. A daily follow-on formula intake of 500ml (17oz) for
a 1–2-year-old and 350ml (12oz) for a child over two years
will provide 60 per cent of his iron requirements for the
day. This can alleviate the stress of trying to get a fussy
child to eat a balanced diet. However, follow-on milks
should not be relied on as your child's only source of iron,
and iron-rich foods should still be continually offered.
Children eating well from the food groups, including the
meat and vegetarian alternative group (see page 16), will be
fine on cow's milk.

Following recent food scares, many families are eating fish
and chicken in preference to red meat, thereby losing out on
red meat's higher iron content. In these families follow-on
formulas can help to make up the deficit in iron intake.

Similarly, children fed on vegetarian diets tend to have a
greater incidence of iron deficiency anaemia, so, once
again, follow-on formulas may be useful to make up the
iron deficit.

Soya formulas

Popular with vegan (see page 148) mothers, soya formulas have
also been used since the early 1980s by mothers hoping to avoid or
treat cow's milk allergy (see page 161). There has always been some
concern over the fact that soya milks contain a form of oestrogen
(the female hormone) and the effect this might have over time. A
recent study on monkeys showed that infant males fed soya formula

had unusual testosterone (male hormone) levels. Another study showed that soya infant formula affected the menstruation of women fed on it when they were babies.

Following reports issued by the Committee on Toxicity of Chemicals in Food, Consumer Products and Food (COT) and the Scientific Advisory Committee on Nutrition (SACN), the Paediatric Group of the British Dietetic Association advises that, as a precaution, use of soya-based infant formulas as first-line treatment for cow's milk allergy should be discouraged during the first six months of life pending further long-term research into their safety. Vegan mothers who are not breast-feeding are the only ones who need to use soya infant formula, as there is no adequate alternative. Infants who do not tolerate formulas based on cow's milk should be fed extensively hydrolysed formulas (speak to your GP or paediatric dietitian for more details on these medically prescribed, specialised formulas).

Goat's milk

Some people believe that goat's milk is better for children who may have, or be susceptible to, a cow's milk allergy. Goat's milk is available fresh and as a powdered infant formula. However, there are no criteria for infant formulas based on goat protein, and it is not suitable for the treatment of allergy in babies (see page 161). Children who are allergic to cow's milk formulas should avoid all mammalian milks, and soya milk too. After one year of age you may give your child goat's milk if you prefer, but do ensure it is pasteurised. If it is not, boil it for two minutes and allow it to cool.

Like cow's milk, goat's milk is low in iron, so between the ages of one and two years, make sure your child drinks no more than 500ml (17oz) per day. After two years of age, he should have no more than 350ml (12oz) per day and eat a balanced diet containing iron-rich foods (see page 38).

Group Two: carbohydrates or starchy foods
Bread, baby cereals, fortified breakfast cereals, oats and other cereals, such as barley or rye, plain and savoury biscuits, potatoes, yams, millet, pasta, semolina and rice.

Major nutrients
This group provides the majority of energy in a child's diet – so important for active minds and bodies. Carbohydrates and starches are good sources of thiamine, niacin, folic acid, vitamin B_6, biotin, zinc and fibre (wholemeal, wholegrain or unprocessed products only).

6-7 months: first tastes
Introduce small amounts of wheat-free, low-fibre (e.g. rice-based) baby cereal, and finely mashed or puréed starchy vegetables, such as potatoes, sweet potatoes, plantain and yams. Rice can be boiled and puréed.

7-9 months: 2-3 portions
Foods can have a more solid, 'lumpy' texture. Start offering finger foods, such as slices of wholemeal toast. Cereals that can be mashed, such as wheat biscuits or oat cereals, can also be offered. Potato and pasta can be mashed or served in pieces for babies to hold and chew. Rice can be mashed. Breadsticks, crackers and rice cakes all make ideal finger foods.

9-12 months: 3-4 portions
Encourage wholemeal products; discourage foods with added sugar, such as biscuits and cakes. Starchy foods should be of a solid texture. All adult cereals, except those with added sugar, honey or chocolate, can be introduced. Try whole pieces of pasta or chopped-up potato. Rice can be boiled. Introduce teacakes, scones, crumpets, English muffins or pancakes.

After one year: minimum of 3-4 portions daily with each meal
Cereals and bread derived from whole grains are richer sources of nutrients and fibre than refined products. Most breakfast cereals are fortified with iron and B vitamins.

Try to offer your child at least one carbohydrate serving, such as one slice of bread, or a small baked potato, or some pasta with a meat, tomato or cheese sauce, at each mealtime.

Do not regularly offer high-fat and high-salt foods, such as pastries, crisps and savoury snacks.

Group Three: vegetables and fruit

Leafy and green vegetables (cabbage, spring greens, kale, cauliflower, Brussels sprouts and broccoli); root vegetables (carrots, swede, turnips); salad vegetables (tomatoes, cucumber), mushrooms, sweetcorn, marrow; fruit (apples, bananas, peaches, oranges, melons) and fruit juices.

Major nutrients

Vitamins A and C, folic acid and fibre, plus a whole host of other health-giving nutrients, such as trace elements and minerals, many of which function as antioxidants (see page 110).

6–7 months: first tastes
(See also Food Allergies page 157)

Introduce purées of soft-cooked vegetables, such as carrot, swede, parsnip, broccoli, cauliflower, peas, sweetcorn and courgette. Babies also generally like puréed fruit, such as cooked apple, ripe pear, banana, peach, mango, plum and melon.

7–9 months: minimum of two portions daily

Introduce raw soft fruit and vegetables, such as banana, melon and tomato, as finger foods. Cooked vegetables and fruit can have a coarser, mashed texture. Do not offer any raw vegetables or hard fruit, such as carrot or apple, because of the risk of choking.

9–12 months: 3–4 portions

Encourage lightly cooked or raw food, chopped or served as finger food. Give some vitamin C-containing fruit or vegetable, or a small amount of diluted orange juice (1:5 ratio of juice to water) with meals (no more than 150ml/5oz of undiluted fruit juice per day), especially if the diet is meat-free. Offer pieces of fruit and vegetables or salad with all meals.

After one year: aim for five portions daily
Encourage unsweetened fruit if vegetables are rejected. Toddlers can cope with food that is more solid, although some fibrous foods, such as celery and radish, may be difficult to eat. Vegetables may be preferred raw, as in grated carrot and chopped tomato, or you might need to disguise them in soups and casseroles. Serve sliced vegetables with sandwiches. Try offering sticks of salad vegetables with a tempting dip or salad dressing. Use fruit in puddings, such as fruit salad, crumbles and pies. Remember that canned and frozen vegetables and fruits can be as nutritious as fresh. Add blended vegetables to soups and casseroles, and to dishes such as cottage pie.

Gina Ford's Top Tip
If your toddler is getting fussy about vegetables, try puréeing soup very smoothly and adding some cool, boiled water or milk to it, then giving it to your toddler to drink from a cup.

Paul Sacher's Top Tip
To improve iron absorption, include some food or drink that contains vitamin C with every meal, e.g. strawberries, kiwi fruit, a small amount (100ml/3¼oz) of pure orange juice or other vitamin C-containing drink.

Q Is 'fresh' always the better option?

A Many people think that fruit and vegetables should be fresh to be healthy, but this not true. Frozen, canned, dried and juice products can sometimes be healthier than the fresh versions, which may have been in cold storage for a lengthy period and gradually lost their vitamin content. Do ask your supermarket or greengrocer how long the particular fruits or vegetables you wish to buy have actually been stored. Canned and frozen produce are often picked and prepared immediately, which locks in the goodness.

Guideline portions for children aged 1–6 years

Food	Portion
Vegetables, raw, cooked, frozen or canned	1 tablespoon
Mixed salad	½ dessert bowl
Apple, pear or banana	½ medium fruit
Melon or pineapple	1 small slice
Apricot, satsuma or kiwi fruit	1 small fruit
Berries or grapes	½ cupful
Fruit salad, fresh, canned or stewed	1–2 tablespoonfuls
Dried fruit	½ tablespoonful
Fruit or vegetable juice	150ml (5oz)

Did you know?

From a nutritional point of view, potatoes are classified as a starchy food, not a vegetable, because they contribute mainly energy to the diet rather than vitamins and minerals.

Q Help! My child won't eat any fruit or vegetables.

A Here are some ideas to include fruit and vegetables in your child's diet.

- Chop some fresh, crunchy vegetables into bite-size portions and serve with a tasty dip, such as hummus, cheese spread, salsa or tzatziki (yoghurt and cucumber dip).

- Slice bananas and add to your child's favourite breakfast cereal, or serve on toast with some peanut butter (see page 106).

- For a quick snack, grill some cheese and tomato on a slice of bread or pitta.

- Include a piece of fruit in your child's packed lunch. If it comes back uneaten day after day, you could try cutting up a variety of fruit and putting it in a small pot with some fruit juice.

- Cook some vegetables, such as carrot, sweetcorn, peas or swede, with potatoes and mash together to make a colourful mixture.

- Stir-fry vegetables with some meat, fish or chicken to make a tasty, Chinese-style meal.

- Add sliced or puréed vegetables to pasta sauces, casseroles or stews.

- Serve some canned fruit (not in syrup) with a yoghurt as a yummy dessert or snack.

- Make a crumble using lots of fruit.

- Serve pancakes with canned or stewed fruit topped with yoghurt or fromage frais.

Alfie, aged 4 years

Problem: Refusal of vegetables

Although Alfie ate well as a baby, he was never very keen on vegetables. During the first stage of weaning, Alfie would fuss and fret when given vegetable purées with his baby rice or sweet potato, but would happily gobble up any type of fruit purée. By the time he reached one year of age he would only ever eat carrots, peas or sweetcorn, and occasionally small amounts of sweet potato. Since he would eat large quantities of these, and ate a wide variety of meats and carbohydrates and masses of fruit, his mother Chrissie was not too concerned about his lack of enthusiasm for other vegetables.

Just before his second birthday, Alfie began to get more and more picky about his food; he started to refuse meals that he had eaten happily before, and he cut out sweet potato and sweetcorn altogether. The only vegetables he would eat now were carrots and peas – and even then he would only eat them if they were smothered with tomato ketchup.

Alfie and his mother led a hectic social life and attended lots of play dates during his second year, which often included lunch or tea. Many of Chrissie's friends were experiencing similar problems of picky eating, and rather than face a massive protest at mealtime from their children, a habit of lunch or tea at McDonalds or Burger King was quickly established.

By the time Alfie reached his third birthday his meals consisted mainly of chicken nuggets or fish fingers served with processed potato shapes and baked beans, carrots or peas with lots of ketchup, or a burger and fries with ketchup on the days they ate out.

His normal breakfast cereal of Weetabix or Shreddies and fruit had also become replaced with cereals, such as Frosties and Coco Pops, which he had discovered during a weekend away with friends.

Although deep down Chrissie was becoming increasingly worried about the limited variety and lack of healthy foods that Alfie was now eating, friends assured her that the majority of children went through this phase and that once Alfie was attending nursery for the full day and eventually going to school, his interest in a large variety of foods would improve.

Chrissie allowed things to continue but, as Alfie neared his fourth birthday, she grew more worried. She had noticed a huge difference in Alfie's behaviour over the previous few months. He had always been a very gentle, easy-going little boy, but now she noticed that he was becoming more and more irritable and much more prone to sudden outbursts of temper, especially at mealtimes. After a particularly difficult morning, followed by a major tantrum at lunchtime, when Chrissie tried to persuade Alfie to try some chicken and pasta bake instead of the usual chicken nuggets or fish fingers, she realised that she was going to have to do something about Alfie's diet. She was convinced that he was not getting all the nutrients he needed from the limited types of foods that he was eating and she was sure that his increasingly bad behaviour was also related to his diet.

That afternoon at a play date she discussed her fears with the other mothers, and one, who had done a Gina Ford consultation the previous year when she had a feeding problem with her 10-month-old baby, suggested that she contact me.

When Chrissie and I spoke, it was obvious that she was distressed and feeling very guilty that she might have done Alfie some damage by allowing him to eat such a restricted diet for so long. I reassured her that while his diet was very limited, I was sure that over a period of several days his nutritional requirements were not as deficient as she thought they were. I told her to continue to feed Alfie as usual but to keep a diary of absolutely everything that he ate and drank over the next four days. It was also important to give exact details of the amounts and the times of everything consumed.

I usually find with young children who eat a very limited diet, and particularly those who refuse to eat vegetables, that they are eating either excessive carbohydrates or protein, which can often contribute to the problem of refusal to eat vegetables and can limit their interest in a wider variety of foods. When Chrissie sent me the food diary, three things immediately stood out. First, Alfie was eating a very generous amount of protein at both lunch and tea; either fish fingers or chicken nuggets, along with a substantial portion of processed potato shapes or oven chips, and baked beans. Although his diet was certainly very limited, Alfie had, over a four-day period, consumed the equivalent of 10 portions of protein per day, when he in fact needed only five portions to meet his daily requirements. Second, taking into account the extra large portions of breakfast cereal and the chips or processed potato shapes that he was having each day, plus the other carbohydrates, he was generally consuming excessive amounts of carbohydrate, which were filling him up. Third, he was eating too few vegetables.

Although an unbalanced diet is not the only cause of poor eating habits or a refusal of vegetables, overloading a child with too much of a particular food group can contribute to the problem. I sent Chrissie a list of foods and information about what constitutes a portion. I advised her that she should not attempt to change Alfie's diet just yet, but to limit the amount of proteins and carbohydrates to the recommended daily amounts (see pages 25 and 7). At the same time, she was to offer him a choice of two vegetables at each meal. I suggested that she and Alfie should go to the shops together and that he should help choose what vegetables he would like for the following two days. It was also important that Chrissie spent time discussing with Alfie why vegetables are important, for example, that carrots will help him to have good eyesight for watching his favourite video, so it is important that he eats a small amount of carrots every week; and broccoli, peppers and cauliflower will help him to grow big and tall like Daddy. I also advised Chrissie to bring colours and shapes into meal preparation, for example, mixing some tiny green peas with some big orange slices of carrot.

During the first week of reintroducing vegetables into Alfie's diet, I advised Chrissie not to be tempted to overload his plate with the same types, even if he showed signs of wanting to eat more. It was better to start off with only two slices of carrot and one broccoli floret and gradually build it up over a period of a couple of weeks than to overload his plate and risk him rejecting it. The majority of children can be persuaded to eat two slices of carrot or one teaspoon of sweetcorn. Every few days it can be increased by such a tiny amount that they rarely notice, and after a couple of weeks they will be happily eating proper portions.

I also explained that it was very important for Chrissie to sit down and eat with Alfie whenever possible. I believe that many eating problems evolve because children reach a stage where they feel very threatened when left sitting alone to eat a plate of food. They cannot understand why they should be expected to eat all the different foods on their plate when Mummy and Daddy are rushing about and only having to eat a sandwich.

Chrissie made a point of always eating breakfast and, whenever possible, eating lunch with Alfie, and within a couple of weeks Alfie had started to eat small amounts of vegetables with his lunch and tea. I felt it was now time to resolve the problem of him wanting to eat only chicken nuggets and fish fingers. I advised her to buy a cookery book called *Easy Peasy* (see page 205), with recipes written especially for children. They should look at the book together and choose a special recipe to cook for Daddy at the weekend. Alfie decided he liked the look of the mini pizza, so on Saturday morning Chrissie helped him to prepare and cook the pizza, reading the recipe out step by step. A quick visit to the kitchen from Daddy, who hinted that he would love some green and red peppers on the top, also went down well and encouraged Alfie to have a small taste of something new.

I advised Chrissie to continue encouraging Alfie to help shop for and prepare a new meal twice a week, once for Daddy and once for his special friends. I also suggested that Chrissie cut out nice pictures of different dishes from magazines and paste them in a scrapbook. It was called 'Alfie's

Special Recipe Book'. Alongside the pictures Chrissie would write simple instructions, which she would read to Alfie as they prepared the meals together. Of course she sometimes had to adapt certain recipes, and sometimes they were given new names. Naming the recipes after characters from your children's favourite video or storybook or a favourite friend or relation will also help to keep their enthusiasm.

It took a further two months for Chrissie to expand on Alfie's range of foods, but she feels all the hard work and effort were worth it as he now eats a healthy diet. Chicken nuggets were replaced by home-made chicken burgers, and fish fingers were replaced with home-made fishcakes. His diet now comprises a wide variety of foods from all the food groups, and each week Chrissie makes a special meal where all the family have to try at least one new food.

While it is important that a child is never forced to eat foods that he genuinely dislikes, I believe that with the huge variety of foods available, particularly vegetables and salads, it is not acceptable that a child dislikes every single one. Refusal of vegetables is a very common problem among young children and can be avoided if parents give their children a choice and refuse to substitute them repeatedly with the same favoured foods.

Group Four: meat and meat alternatives
Meat, poultry, eggs, fish, lentils, peas, beans, nuts and soya.

Major nutrients
Energy (calories) mainly from fat, protein, iron, zinc, B vitamins (B_{12} in animal foods only).

For portion advice, refer to the protein information on page 24.

6–7 months: first tastes
Puréed lamb, beef, pork, chicken, turkey and fish (e.g. cod, salmon, tuna). Meat alternatives, such as puréed pulses (lentils, peas, beans).

7-9 months: one portion

Introduce soft-cooked, coarsely puréed or minced meat, fish or pulses. Serve casseroles and stews, to which you can add some mashed pulses.

9-12 months: minimum of one portion daily

This age group needs a daily minimum of one serving of animal protein or two of vegetable protein. Use home-cooked meat, fish and chicken, and try to avoid too many processed foods, such as sausages, burgers, fish fingers, fishcakes and chicken nuggets. In a vegetarian diet use a mixture of different pulses and starchy foods, such as baked beans with toast, or dhal and rice (see page 146). Try reduced-sugar-and-salt baked beans, as well as other pulses.

After one year: minimum of two portions daily

Encourage low-fat meat, such as chicken and turkey. Children often prefer meat to be soft and moist, so try serving it with a salt-free gravy or sauce. Serve white fish, such as cod and haddock, as well as the oily fishes, such as sardines, herrings and mackerel (the fat in fish has been shown to promote a strong immune system). Try using mashed sardines, tuna, cold meat and peanut butter as sandwich fillers. **Do not give whole nuts to children under five years of age because there is a risk of choking. If your child or family has a history of food allergy, asthma, eczema or hay fever, avoid giving peanut butter until three years of age** (see page 106). Pulses, such as lentils, chickpeas and beans, are great in casseroles and stews.

Group Five: occasional foods

Cakes, sweet biscuits, sweetened squash, sweetened desserts and milk drinks, cream, ice cream, sugar, jam, honey, crisps, savoury snacks, fried and fatty foods.

Note that none of these foods is necessary in your baby's diet. Having too much of them can eventually lead to weight problems and high blood pressure as they contain a lot of fat, sugar and salt. Try not to offer foods from this group regularly.

6-9 months

Babies naturally love sweet foods, but it is very important not to succumb to their demands, and to ensure that they eat savoury foods in addition to naturally sweet ones, such as fruit-based solids. Fruit juices contain sugar and are not necessary, so if you do give them try to restrict them to mealtimes to protect teeth. Use very diluted pure fruit juice, and give no more than 150ml (5oz) per day.

9-12 months

Use moderate amounts of butter and margarine, and small amounts of jam on bread. Try to avoid salty foods.

After one year

Limit crisps and savoury snacks. Give your child fruit yoghurts, cheese or bread if he is hungry between meals. Do not add sugar to drinks. Try to limit soft drinks to mealtimes, or avoid them altogether. Encourage a pattern of three meals plus 2–3 healthy snacks each day. Discourage frequent snacking on fatty or sugary foods.

Some healthy snacks

Snack	Nutrients
Wholegrain toast fingers with margarine or butter	B group vitamins, fibre, vitamins A, D and E
Yoghurt, fromage frais, cheese triangles	Calcium, protein, B group vitamins, zinc
Fortified non-sugary breakfast cereal and milk	A range of vitamins and minerals, plus iron
Fresh fruit cut into hand-size pieces	Vitamin C, fibre and folic acid

The myth about junk food

There is no such thing as junk food, only a junk diet. For example, many people regard chocolate as a junk food, but it actually contains some useful nutrients, such as calcium, protein and energy, which are all essential for a growing child. The problem occurs when chocolate and other foods high in sugar and fat are eaten to excess and displace more nutritious foods from the other food groups. If chocolate or crisps are eaten occasionally along with items from the major food groups, they are not detrimental to a child's health.

Try not to use high-fat and high-sugar foods as rewards or treats, or you could be laying the foundations for lifelong unhealthy eating. It is far better to reward good behaviour with activities, such as trips to the park or the zoo, or items that promote activity, such as a ball or bicycle.

Avoid telling your children that foods are good or bad. This could lead to them rejecting 'good' foods and wanting 'bad' ones more than ever. Promote a balanced diet, including many different types of food. If children won't eat something, try offering it again later. Research has shown that it can take up to 12 attempts before children will accept a new taste.

Anya, aged 2 years and 10 months

Problem: Fantastic feeder to fussy feeder

Cause: Over-compensating for likes and dislikes

Sophie first contacted me when Anya was three months old. She had been sleeping according to the Contented Baby Routines but, following a holiday when the family were travelling around France, she started waking every two or three hours. After a week-long consultation, Anya was back to sleeping 12 hours a night.

Anya continued to be an excellent sleeper and, when weaned, she took really well to solids. Sophie experimented successfully with a whole range of foods, which she prepared herself. Anya's favourites were spinach and potato, liver, shepherd's pie, and cod with sweet potato.

Sophie went back to work when Anya was six months old and a nanny took over. Anya continued to eat well and with great enthusiasm. Sophie recollects that she used to look fairly disdainfully on those friends whose babies wouldn't eat anything that didn't come out of a jar. Anya, in fact, was the opposite: the one thing she wouldn't eat was food from a jar.

As Anya got older she continued to prefer 'mushy' foods, such as shepherd's pie, but generally she remained a good eater, and Sophie did not see this as a problem. Then Sophie decided to give up work when Anya was around 20 months old. The nanny left and Anya's eating habits seemed to change overnight. To Sophie's surprise, in the first couple of weeks when she had sole care of her daughter, Anya began to refuse some of her meals. Initially, she would eat a little before pushing the spoon away, but the problem became more pronounced and Anya began constantly to refuse her meals. Sophie responded by becoming increasingly anxious. The nanny had been hugely competent, and Sophie felt that on some level her daughter must be reacting to the change in routine, as she persisted in refusing the wide range of foods she had formerly enjoyed. Sophie tried to entice Anya to eat by pretending the spoon was an aeroplane. She would offer her alternatives if one of the favourite foods was rejected. Within a fortnight of the nanny's departure, Sophie had resorted to giving the few foods Anya was now prepared to eat – yoghurt and grated cheese. Mealtimes became increasingly upsetting, with Anya pushing the foods onto the floor and Sophie almost crying with frustration.

Within two months it had reached a stage where Anya was eating only Weetabix with banana, jam sandwiches, biscuits, chocolate and ice cream. Sophie did occasionally try to withdraw biscuits between meals, but Anya would cry and scream until Sophie gave in. It would be the same at other people's houses, which in the end made it very stressful for Sophie to go out anywhere with Anya. The less good food Anya ate, the more she demanded biscuits and cried until she got them. Sophie would give in and then

Anya was not hungry at mealtimes. She would be hungry again later and demand more sweet things. Sophie couldn't get herself out of the habit of giving in to Anya's demands for biscuits and chocolates, and at this point she rang me for advice.

When I spoke to Sophie I said that it was of the utmost importance to get rid of all biscuits, sweets and ice cream from the house and to decide firmly that there must be no eating between meals. We prepared a menu plan for the next seven days and I told Sophie that if Anya cried and screamed for biscuits and sweets when she was given her meals, she was to walk away from her. She must not get into a conversation about food.

Sophie started the plan at the weekend so that her husband could support her. I suggested that they offer Anya a selection of fruits and yoghurt at breakfast instead of the usual Weetabix and banana. I explained that we should save the foods that we knew Anya would eat until teatime. We did not want her final meal of the day before bedtime to become a battle. By offering only fruit and yoghurt at breakfast, Anya would, we hoped, be hungrier for lunch. Lunch was always her worst meal, where she played up the most, refusing all forms of protein for the last five months. I suggested that Sophie shouldn't overburden Anya with huge platefuls of food, but put small amounts, including some new vegetables, on the plate.

Sophie recognised with hindsight that her concern about her daughter missing the nanny had meant she had reacted too quickly to Anya's altered feeding habits. We both agreed that Anya, a bright little girl, had rapidly established that fussy eating was rewarded by her mother's undivided attention. At 21 months of age she began to manipulate her mother with great success. The more Sophie responded, the more the pattern was set. Sugary snacks between meals ruined Anya's appetite and made it even less likely that she would eat wholesome food.

Reversing these patterns was going to be challenging for Anya's parents. Having been used to getting her own way, Anya had awful tantrums during the first three days. She demanded biscuits, hurled herself onto the floor and vehemently refused her meals. It was very upsetting for her parents. Anya's sleep was starting to be affected – she was waking earlier and, as a consequence, was whingy and prone to tears during most of the first few days. However, Sophie and her husband persevered and, to their delight, by the fourth morning, Anya ate her fruit and yoghurt within eight minutes. At lunchtime, within 20 minutes she happily ate fish fingers and peas with baby new potatoes. The pattern was broken.

Gradually, over the next few days, they reintroduced cereal and toast at breakfast time. Once they became confident that her lunchtime appetite had returned, they were able to increase her breakfast.

I encouraged her parents to give her nutritious finger foods at lunchtime, including cooked carrot batons, pieces of chicken breast, honey-roast ham and cheesy fingers. By doing this, Anya was able to feed herself, and while she was no longer in a position to choose her meals, she did have a level of control that pacified her. In addition, I told Sophie to praise her when she ate, but to ignore her if the food was either rejected or thrown from the high chair. Within the first week, Anya's diet had improved enormously. She was eating a very good breakfast, including porridge, toast fingers and cut-up fruit. Her lunch had the appropriate balance of nutritious food. By the second week she was happily attempting to feed herself most of the meal using her fingers, and she was also allowing her mother to help. On the increasingly rare occasions when food was refused, Sophie responded by making no fuss, but offering no alternatives. Her daughter's stamina was improved, she no longer needed or expected sugary snacks between meals, and on the occasions when they were out the only snacks she was allowed were healthy ones in moderation – fruit, raisins and raw vegetables.

Toddlers are very sensitive to the response their behaviour generates. While Anya's response was extreme, it was clearly motivated by her discovery that she could get her mother's attention by not eating. Her mother's lack of confidence in herself meant that she over-compensated for her daughter's fussy eating. Fortunately, they both re-established good feeding patterns, which they have been able to maintain to this day.

Anya is now five and she eats a wide range of foods. She gets no choice of lunch at school or at home, which I believe is a good thing.

Essential Nutrients – the Building Blocks for a Healthy Life

Q What nutrients does my child need and how can I be sure that he is getting everything he needs?

A Children are not mini-adults. In the early years and during puberty they are growing faster than at any other time of their lives, so their requirements are different from those of adults.

The essential nutrients can be summarised as follows: protein, carbohydrate, fat, vitamins, minerals and trace elements. It is not necessary to know exactly which foods provide which nutrients, but ensuring that your child's diet provides the correct balance of foods containing these important elements is essential for a healthy life.

So how do you know if your child is getting everything

he needs? The simple answer is to become familiar with the food groups explained earlier (see page 1), then all you need do is follow our recommendations on the amounts needed from each food group and you can be guaranteed that your child is getting everything he needs.

However, do remember that our recommendations are average amounts and that children are individuals: some will eat more and others will eat less. Similarly, do not worry if your child eats far less or much more on a particular day – it is the average amount consumed that is important.

Did you know?

There is now scientific evidence demonstrating that babies who miss out on adequate nutrition during the first year of life have lower IQs than babies who were properly nourished.

Protein

Protein is the building block of the body, so your child must get enough of this important nutrient in order to grow. Protein is found mainly in animal foods, such as meat, poultry, fish and dairy products (milk, cheese, eggs), and also in some vegetable foods, such as pulses (lentils, peas, beans). If your child is following a vegetarian diet, please refer to Chapter 3. As growth is most rapid in childhood, it is crucial that adequate amounts of protein are eaten. Imagine trying to build a house and not having enough bricks – it would not be a very strong house at all.

Make sure your child eats enough of the main protein-containing foods (Groups One and Four) and the chances are he will be getting enough protein.

Q How much protein does my baby or child need each day?

A The table below will help you to ensure that your child gets enough protein to grow well and develop strong, healthy muscles. (A portion of protein equals roughly 3g.)

Age	Portions of protein needed per day
0–6 months	4
7 months–3 years	5
4–6 years	7

Examples of a portion of protein

- ½ a standard-size egg
- 240ml (8oz) of breast milk
- 210ml (7oz) of infant formula
- 90ml (3oz) of cow's milk
- ½ a pot of yoghurt
- 1 small hot-dog sausage
- Small piece of cooked chicken (size of chicken nugget)
- ⅓ of a beefburger
- Small piece of cod, (size of 1 fish finger)
- Small piece of cheese (size of ½ matchbox)
- 1 large slice of salami
- Thin spread of peanut butter
- 3 tablespoons of cooked lentils
- 4–5 tablespoons of baked beans
- ½ rasher of unsalted, unsmoked bacon

For example, a six-year-old needs seven portions of protein per day. If he eats an egg for breakfast, some cod (the size of two fish fingers) and a pot of yoghurt for lunch, and a hot-dog sausage for dinner, he will meet his requirements, as this amounts to seven portions of protein.

Remember, even if children don't eat the recommended amount of protein in a single day, this is no cause for concern as they will often make it up over the next few days. Remember, too, that diets in the Western world generally contain more than enough protein. If your child is drinking the recommended amount of milk (see page 2), or eating adequate amounts from the protein-containing food groups, he is likely to be getting all the protein he needs.

Carbohydrate

Also known as starch, carbohydrate supplies energy, the fuel for our bodies. Without enough carbohydrate, children run out of energy and do not perform as well as they should. That's why eating breakfast, which is generally a carbohydrate-rich meal, is extremely important. Young children who are sleepy and bad-tempered during the morning or late afternoon might be eating either the wrong types of carbohydrate or simply not enough.

Improve your child's carbohydrate intake

Offer any of the following foods to keep your child well fuelled throughout the day.

- Any type of bread – brown, high-fibre white or wholegrain (avoid giving babies bread containing large grains).
- Breakfast cereals, but choose non-sweetened, unprocessed types, such as muesli or oats.
- Any type of rice – white or brown (wholegrain rice has a nice, nutty flavour).
- Potatoes and sweet potatoes (try grilling thin strips brushed with olive oil as an alternative to chips).
- Any type of pasta, such as spaghetti or macaroni.

Try to ensure you provide some form of carbohydrate at every meal. If a child is not eating enough, his weight gain is likely to be poor. It is very rare for healthy children not to eat enough carbohydrate.

Make sure your child eats daily from the Group Two foods listed earlier (see page 7) and he will be getting enough carbohydrate.

Q What are the best types of carbohydrate?

A Not all carbohydrates are created equal. The process of refining strips foods of many of their micronutrients. For example, processing wholegrain wheat into white flour removes the husk, which is rich in B vitamins. If your child lives on a diet of white bread, white pasta, crisps and little else, he is unlikely to be getting the right balance of micronutrients. Carbohydrates that have been stripped of all their goodness, e.g. crisps, biscuits, and sweets, are often referred to as 'empty calories' as they provide little in the diet other than energy.

Another drawback of refined foods is that they are digested and absorbed very quickly. The body breaks carbohydrates down into glucose (a sugar), which is the substance that fuels all the body's processes, including the functions of the brain. Refined foods are converted rapidly into glucose, giving a sharp rise in blood sugar. These high levels of sugar trigger the body to pump the hormone insulin into the blood. Insulin causes excessive sugar in the diet to be stored in the cells as fat, so it has been suggested that refined foods are playing a significant part in increasing the levels of childhood obesity. If a small amount of refined carbohydrate is included as part of a balanced diet, this should not cause a problem.

Inevitably, a rapid rise in blood sugar from eating excessive refined carbohydrate, followed by a dip in blood sugar caused by insulin doing its job, can affect the way children behave and their ability to concentrate.

This roller-coaster effect can be avoided by eating fewer refined foods, and more of those which are digested more slowly and keep blood sugar levels more constant. Mood swings and unruly behaviour followed by periods of grumpiness or sleepiness may all be signs that your child is sensitive to these rises and drops in blood sugar.

Unrefined carbohydrates, such as wholegrain bread, brown rice and wholemeal pasta, are definitely best for children, so try introducing them slowly by 1–2 years of age and, with any luck, your child will be happy to eat them as he gets older. Also, whenever possible, avoid pre-prepared foods, and serve freshly cooked ingredients to give your child the healthiest carbohydrates.

Maltodextrins

Produced from any source of starch, including corn, potato and rice, maltodextrins are partially broken-down sugars. In the food industry they are used in low-fat dressings, coffee whiteners, some artificial sweeteners and, more alarmingly, many savoury baby foods. (They are also turned into glue that is used on envelopes and stamps.)

Maltodextrins are not found naturally in foods: they occur only as additives and provide nothing but energy. They do, however, enhance the flavour and mouth feel of foods, and are cheap to produce, so manufacturers like to use them. However, in one test on a baby jar of meat casserole, the level of maltodextrin was higher than the actual meat content.

We do not yet know the effects of sensitising babies to the taste and mouth feel of maltodextrin on later food preferences, but we do know it is unwise to fill children up on empty calories that provide energy but no other nutritional benefit. Our advice is to avoid baby foods that contain maltodextrins. Always read labels carefully to ensure you are giving your baby the best food possible (see page 106).

Dental caries

Despite improved health education, dental caries is still common among children in the UK. It is caused by excessive intake of sweet foods and drinks, and poor dental hygiene. Babies who have sweet drinks from a bottle, particularly at bedtime, are most at risk of tooth decay because the liquid stays in contact with the teeth for longer while the child falls asleep. After six months of age bottles should not be used for feeding, but if they are introduced, try to offer children drinks from an open cup by six months of age before their teeth start to come through.

Once your baby starts developing teeth, introduce him to the taste of toothpaste on your finger and let him play with his own toothbrush. Your local clinic or health visitor will probably supply you with free samples at the developmental checks at 6–9 months, 24 months and four years. Offer a children's toothpaste with a child-friendly taste, and encourage him to play with the brush in his mouth and even to suck it. Encourage brushing twice a day, after breakfast and before bedtime. Between meals, encourage tooth-friendly snacks, such as cheese or fruit. Try to avoid sugary drinks, including fruit juices, and encourage milk or water only.

Fibre

Also known as 'roughage', fibre is an essential part of the diet, responsible for keeping things moving and preventing constipation. It also feeds the bacteria that live in the digestive tract, which in turn produce substances that keep the gut healthy. Young babies do not have any fibre in their diet, and that is why their stools are generally loose and runny. Once weaning begins and fibre is introduced, the consistency of their stools changes.

Fibre is found only in plant foods, so a diet low in fruit, vegetables and wholegrains will not only lack vitamins and minerals, but will also be low in fibre, which can lead to constipation (see page 167). Fibre should be increased gradually in children's diets, and high-fibre diets should be avoided until at least five years of age (see page 145).

Fibre content of some common foods

Low fibre	High fibre
'Smooth' fruit juice, with no pulp or bits of fruit	Fruit juice with pulp or bits of fruit
Sweets and chocolate	Raisins or fruit, e.g. apple, banana, orange
White rice	Brown or wholegrain rice
White pasta	Wholemeal pasta
Baked products using white flour	Baked products using wholemeal flour
White bread	Wholemeal, wholegrain or granary bread
Processed cereal, e.g. puffed rice or cornflakes	Wholewheat cereal biscuit, high-fibre/ fruit cereals
	Vegetables
	Pulses (peas, beans and lentils)

Fat

For many of us the thought of fat has very negative connotations. We know that too much fat can be bad for us and lead to weight problems and even coronary heart disease. This is true, but children are very different from adults, and have very different nutritional requirements.

Fat is 'liquid gold': per gram it has the highest energy content in our diets, so, like carbohydrate, it helps to fuel our bodies. If we have too much fuel, our bodies store it as fat, which is not ideal if you are an adult; but if you are a child, this fuel is crucial to power the rapid growth and development that is occurring. For this reason, almost half of breast milk is fat. If your child is underweight, try melting butter over vegetables, and don't be afraid to fry foods. If you are at all concerned about your child's weight, contact your health visitor or GP.

Another good reason for including fats in the diet is that they contain vitamins A, D, E and K: in fact, these vitamins are found only in fat-containing foods, so diets very low in fat are likely to be low in these vitamins. Essential Fatty Acids (EFAs) are found in breast and formula milks and foods containing fat. EFAs are essential for a strong immune system. LCPs (long chain polyunsaturated fatty acids) are found naturally in breast milk and play an important role in the development of the brain and eyesight. For this reason, infant formulas should contain LCPs in order to give babies the best start in life. Similarly, omega-3 fatty acids, found in fish oils and some vegetables oils, are important for the development of a strong immune system.

Sources of fat

Fats can be divided into two main types: those derived from animals and those from plants. The general rule to remember is that vegetable fats are healthier in the long term than animal fats (with the exception of fish fats, which have valuable health benefits).

Fat source	Type of fat	Form and uses
Meat (beef, lamb, pork) and poultry (chicken, turkey)	Saturated	Usually solid (butter, lard, block margarine); used for baking; also found in milk, cheese and other dairy products
Dark fish (salmon, sardines) and white fish (cod, haddock)	Polyunsaturated	Found mainly in fish itself (dark fish has more than white)
Vegetable oils (corn, safflower, sunflower)	Polyunsaturated	Often liquid, used for cooking, but also used to make soft margarines
Vegetable oils (olive, rapeseed)	Monounsaturated	Liquid, used for cooking, but also used in soft margarines
Vegetable oils (coconut, palm)	Saturated	Liquid or in blocks
Nuts and seeds (walnuts, sesame and sunflower seeds)	Polyunsaturated	Solid (nut butters); sometimes liquid (salad oil); also used whole, chopped or ground in cakes, biscuits and bread
Nuts and seeds (almonds, hazelnuts)	Monosaturated	As above

Paul Sacher's Top Tip
Although some fats are healthier than others, they all contain the same number of calories per gram, so can contribute equally to excessive weight gain.

Vitamins, minerals and trace elements

Most of us are familiar with the main vitamins – A, B, C, D and E – and minerals, such as calcium for bones and iron to carry oxygen around in the blood. But not everyone is as aware of the trace elements, such as selenium, copper and zinc, that are required to help our bodies run smoothly. (These three minerals act as antioxidants, see page 110.)

Keeping tabs on the amount of trace elements your child is eating would be virtually impossible, so how can you ensure your child is getting enough? These nutrients are contained in all the food groups described earlier (see page 1), so it is important to make sure your child eats food from all the groups. A child who does not eat fruit or vegetables, for example, would be lacking in many vitamins, minerals and trace elements, and a child not eating carbohydrates, such as bread and rice, could be missing out on the essential B vitamins.

If you are concerned that your child is not eating a balanced and varied diet, it may be beneficial to give him a multivitamin and mineral supplement recommended for children. These are available in liquid or chewable tablet form, or as capsules for older children. Ask your pharmacist or a dietitian for advice if you are unsure which one to use. Always follow the recommended dosage on the container. Offer the supplement daily for one month, then stop for one month to prevent any unnecessary build-up of vitamins and minerals in the body. Use the supplement only while you are concerned about your child's diet, and try to follow the advice in this book to improve areas of concern.

The Department of Health (D.H) recommends supplementing with vitamins A, C and D only rather than a complete multivitamin and mineral supplement. These are available from health centres and baby clinics. The following guidelines are useful in deciding when to use the D.H vitamin supplement:

- Breast-fed babies from mothers with a good diet during pregnancy need supplementation from six months of age.

- If the mother's diet was not particularly balanced during pregnancy, supplementation should start at one month.

- Bottle-fed infants who drink more than 500ml (17oz) of infant or follow-on formula a day do not need vitamin supplements because the infant formulas are fortified with vitamin D.

- At one year of age all infants should be given supplements as insurance against a poor intake at a time when it is hard to be certain that the diet provides an adequate amount.

- Vitamin supplements should be continued until five years of age, unless the diet is diverse and plentiful.

Make sure you do not double up on supplements, i.e. by giving the D.H recommended ones as well as another brand containing the same vitamins. Excessive levels of vitamins A and D can accumulate to toxic levels in the body.

Did you know?
Even though vitamins and minerals are extremely important, they are needed in only tiny amounts – milligrams (mg) or micrograms (mcg).

Vitamin C
Vitamin C is essential for the growth and repair of body cells, helps white blood cells to fight infection and also acts as an antioxidant

(see page 110), essential for good health. It is not stored in the body, so foods containing vitamin C need to be eaten regularly.

Q **What are good sources of vitamin C?**

A Some of the best sources of vitamin C are fruits (especially citrus fruit and juice), kiwi fruit and strawberries, green vegetables and tomatoes.

Q **How many portions of vitamin C-containing foods does my child need?**

Age	Portions required per day*
0–12 months	5
1–6 years	6

* One portion equals approximately 5mg

Vitamin C content of some common foods

Food	Approximate portions of vitamin C
1 orange segment	2
1 apricot	1½
Small bunch of grapes	2½
½ medium kiwi fruit	3
1 small slice of canteloupe melon	3
1 large slice of pineapple	3
30ml (1oz) of apple juice with added vitamin C	2
30ml (1oz) of orange juice	3
½ broccoli spear	3
1 small slice of red pepper	3
1 small raw tomato	2
1 tablespoon of peas	1
1 tablespoon of mashed potato	1

Note: The above table demonstrates how easy it is to obtain the recommended amount of vitamin C from diet. Do not be fooled into buying artificial drinks that claim to be good sources of vitamin C.

Paul Sacher's Top Tip
Vitamin C is destroyed by heat, and it can also leach out into water if vegetables are soaked before cooking or cooked in too much liquid. To preserve the maximum amount of vitamin C in foods, make sure you steam, microwave or stir-fry them.

Vitamin D
Essential for the body to make strong bones, vitamin D is produced mainly by the action of sunlight on the skin. A dietary source is not usually necessary. The exact amount of vitamin D required has never been calculated because the amount produced when sun hits the skin is difficult to measure.

Q What are good sources of vitamin D?

A The main source is sunlight, but in countries where people are covered up and have little exposure to the sun, vitamin D must be obtained from the diet. It is found in margarine, butter, full-fat milk, evaporated milk, eggs, oily fish and liver.

Paul Sacher's Top Tip
Vitamin D is the most toxic of all vitamins, so supplements containing high levels should not be taken for prolonged periods.

Q How much vitamin D does my child need?

A After three years of age most children do not require a
dietary source of vitamin D. However, if your child does
not get much exposure to the sun, he should continue on a
supplement containing 7mcg of vitamin D per day.

Calcium

Calcium is a mineral essential for the development of bones and
teeth.

Q What are good sources of calcium?

A The main sources of calcium are milk, dairy products
and milk substitutes (see page 1). Calcium from animal
sources is absorbed well by the body, but it can also be
obtained from pulses (peas, beans and lentils), green
leafy vegetables, dried fruit, nuts and seeds, canned fish
and products made with fortified flour.

Q How many portions of calcium-rich foods does my child
need?

Age	Portions required per day*
Under 1 year	10
1–3 years	7
4–6 years	9
Pregnant women aged 19–50	14
Breast-feeding mothers	25

* One portion of calcium equals roughly 50mg.

Note: Pregnant women and breast-feeding mothers may require a calcium supplement to ensure they meet the necessary calcium requirement.

Calcium content of some common foods

Food	Approximate portions of calcium
Glass of milk (210ml/7oz)	5
Infant formula milk (210ml/7oz)	2
Piece of Cheddar cheese, matchbox size (30g/1oz)	4
1 tablespoon of grated Cheddar	1
Large cheese spread triangle (30g/1oz)	2
Small pot of cottage cheese (110g/4oz)	2
Cream cheese in a sandwich (30g/1oz)	1
Pot of yoghurt (150g/5oz)	4
Pot of fromage frais (100g/3½oz)	2
1 scoop of ice cream (60g/2oz)	2
Custard made with milk (120g/4½oz)	3
Milk pudding (200g/7oz)	5
3 slices of white, brown or wholemeal bread	2
1 plain digestive biscuit (15g/½oz)	1
Cooked broccoli (90g/3oz)	½
Cooked spinach (45g/1½oz)	1½
Small can of baked beans (150g/5oz)	1½
2 tablespoons canned red kidney beans (60g/2oz)	1
Orange (160g/5¼oz)	1½
Dried apricots (60g/2oz)	1
Plain peanuts (60g/2oz)	½
Canned sardines in tomato sauce (100g/3½oz)	9
Canned salmon without bones (100g/3½oz)	2
Shelled prawns (60g/2oz)	2
Cheese and egg quiche (150g/5oz)	7
Macaroni cheese (200g/7oz)	7½

Iron

Iron is essential for healthy red blood cells, which transport oxygen around the body. Children who do not take in sufficient amounts of iron are at risk of developing anaemia (see page 164), which causes tiredness, poor concentration, irritability and an overall lack of energy and enthusiasm.

Q What are good sources of iron?

A Red meat is the best source of iron in the diet, but offal, such as liver and kidney, and oily fish, such as sardines, are also high in iron. Other good sources include eggs (which should be cooked until both the yolk and white are solid), beans and lentils, breakfast cereals and baby foods fortified with iron, dried fruit, broccoli, and green leafy vegetables.

Paul Sacher's Top Tip

Iron is easily absorbed from meat, but less so from other foods. Consuming something rich in vitamin C alongside iron-containing foods increases the body's absorption of the iron, so try to serve iron and vitamin C combinations, such as lentil casserole and orange juice. (See page 34 for a list of foods containing vitamin C.)

Q How much iron does my child need?

Age	Iron portions required per day*
0–3 months	3½
4–6 months	8½
7–11 months	15½
1–3 years	14
4–6 years	12
Breast-feeding woman	15

* One portion of iron equals roughly 0.5mg.

Iron content of some common foods

Food	Approximate portions of iron
1 Weetabix (20g/⅔oz)	3
Special K (20g/⅔oz)	5½
Full-fat cow's milk (110ml/3½oz)	negligible
Boiled egg (60g/2oz)	2
Unsalted or unsmoked bacon rasher (60g/2oz)	1
Beef mince (60g/2oz)	3
Sausage (60g/2oz)	2
Fish fingers (120g/4½oz)	2
Chicken, white and dark meat (60g/2oz)	1
Cod steak, grilled (60g/2oz)	½
1 slice wholemeal bread (30g/1oz)	1½
Lentils (60g/2oz)	2½
Broccoli, cooked (30g/1oz)	½
Dried mixed fruit (30g/1oz)	1

Note: Remember that iron is absorbed much better from animal foods than from plant foods.

Salt

While salt is added to many foods to give flavour, too much of it can be very dangerous for babies and can lead to high blood pressure, strokes and heart disease later in life. It is important to raise your child on a diet that does not contain excessive salt, as habits learnt in childhood will continue into adulthood.

The Food Standards Agency recommends not exceeding the following intakes of salt for children:

Age	Maximum salt intake per day
0–6 months	less than 1g
7–12 months	1g
1–3 years	2g
4–6 years	3g

The current levels of salt intake for children aged four years and older are higher than the recommended levels. In fact, children's salt consumption is relatively higher than that of adults for their weight. This is a cause of concern because a taste for salt developed in childhood can cause numerous health problems in adulthood.

Q How can I reduce salt levels in my child's diet?

A
- Reduce the amount of salt added during cooking and at the table.
- Flavour food with herbs and spices instead of salt.
- Do not leave a salt-cellar on the table during meals.
- Three-quarters of the salt we eat is from processed foods, so it is important to check the salt content on food labels (see page 109).
- Restrict salty foods, such as crisps, nuts, packet soups and sauces, and convenience meals.

Gina Ford's Feeding Plan: 1–3 years

During the second year the rate at which a child grows slows down considerably and many parents notice a sudden decrease in their child's appetite. A pattern often emerges where a child will eat masses one day, then very little for a couple of days. This is all quite normal and it is important that you have a clear understanding of what your toddler needs to eat from each of the food groups and what a portion consists of in order to meet his nutritional needs. It is also important that you calculate your toddler's overall intake during several days and not on a daily basis. Keeping a food diary should help eliminate any concerns you are having and help prevent problems of fussy feeding, which are often caused by anxious parents resorting to cajoling and force-feeding because they are concerned that their toddler is not eating enough.

- Milk still plays an important role in helping to provide your child with a healthy, well-balanced diet, but during the second year solids should gradually become his main source of nutrition. If you allow your baby to continue drinking his milk from a bottle after one year, you may find that he becomes fussier at mealtimes and even starts refusing to eat at all at some meals. To avoid this happening it is important that all drinks are given from a cup and that the bottle is abandoned completely.

- During this stage the daily recommendation is 500ml (17oz) for 1–2 year olds and 350ml (12oz) for children over two years old, but this doesn't need to be drunk as milk, and can include other dairy products such as yoghurt. If you aim to give a drink of 150–180ml (5–6oz) first thing in the morning and last thing at night, with an optional drink of 90–120ml (3–4oz) at teatime, along with any milk in his cereal, you can be confident that your toddler will be getting enough milk, but not so much that his appetite for solids would be affected. If he likes more milk in the morning or evening, it is fine to give him more than I recommend, but you may have to give him water or well-diluted juice with his tea if his interest in solids decreases.

- After one year your toddler can be given full-fat cow's milk, and after two years half-fat (semi-skimmed) milk can be introduced. If you find that he is getting fussy about milk or refusing it altogether, ensure that he gets extra cheese, yoghurts, and meals where milk and cheese are added to the ingredients. When choosing yoghurts, try to avoid the types of fromage frais that are high in sugar. Many brands are recommended for children by the manufacturers, but some can have as much as 14.5g (3 teaspoons) of sugar in a 100g (3½oz) pot. Try to stick to natural yoghurt, adding your own mashed or puréed fruit.

- Your toddler still needs 3–4 helpings of carbohydrates a day. He should now be taking more of these in the form of finger foods, such as mini sandwiches, breadsticks and pizza.

- Your toddler should also have 3–4 helpings of vegetables and fruits, with more vegetables than fruit. After one year nearly all his fruit and vegetables should be served chopped, sliced or diced instead of puréed. But if he gets fussy about vegetables, it is better to purée them in a sauce or soup rather than give them up altogether. Salad vegetables and raw vegetables should also be offered on a regular basis.

- If under two, your child needs one serving of animal protein (if over two years of age he needs two servings of animal protein) or 2–3 servings of vegetable protein a day. He should be encouraged to have this finely chopped or cut into small pieces rather than mashed or puréed. Continue to avoid meats, such as ham and bacon, that are high in salt, until your child is over two years.

- Continue to offer your toddler a variety of different foods, but do not make a fuss or force him to eat more than he wants. If he eats less at one meal, he will certainly eat more at another meal over the next few days. Try not to get into the habit of bribing him with unhealthy puddings or sweets to finish his meal. Bribery of this sort nearly always ends up with mealtimes becoming a battle of wills, with the child usually winning.

- The timing of meals plays an important part in maintaining healthy eating habits. Toddlers use up a lot of energy and are still prone to becoming overtired very quickly. Schedule meals at regular times and stick to them. Try to continue giving the main protein meal at lunchtime so that you can be more relaxed about his tea if he becomes tired and fussy later in the day.

- Schedule snacks and drinks so that they are not being given too close to mealtimes. Allowing a two-hour gap and offering healthy snacks and well-diluted juice or water should ensure that your child's appetite is not affected.

- Self-feeding should be encouraged during the second year, even if it does become messy. You will also have to allow slightly longer at mealtimes when your child starts to feed himself. However, still allow only a certain time for meals: do not allow them to drag on for lengthy periods if he is not interested in eating and particularly if he starts playing with his food, or throwing it on the floor.

- Children learn by example, so try to eat with your child every day. He will learn how to use his cutlery and how to behave at mealtimes much faster if he is allowed to eat along with adults in a happy, relaxed environment. By two years of age he should have mastered the art of using a small spoon and fork to eat all his meals without assistance.

Between the ages of one and three, a typical day's feeding plan may look something like the following:

7–7.30am   Drink of full-fat milk
Choice of cereals or oats with chopped fresh fruit *or*
Toast and spreads or toasted muffins *or*
Fresh fruit and yoghurt *or*
Scrambled eggs or boiled eggs with toast *or*
Baked beans on toast

9.30–10am   Drink of well-diluted juice or water
Small piece of fresh fruit or rice cakes or breadsticks

12–1pm   Expand on the recipes that you have been giving your toddler, adapting them to more adult versions and introducing recipes eaten by the rest of the family. For example:
Meatballs in tomato sauce with diced potatoes, diced peppers and sweetcorn
Salmon and broccoli bake served with chopped green beans and carrots
Liver casserole with sautéd potatoes and chopped cabbage
Chicken and mushroom stir-fry
Grilled lamb chops with mashed potato and courgettes in a tomato sauce
Chicken and noodles
Mini salmon skewers with potatoes, butternut squash and broccoli florets
Chicken and butter-bean burgers served with salad and home-made chips

Mediterranean grilled vegetables with tomato rice

Avocado and cheese salad with sautéd potatoes

Butter-beans with tomato and rice risotto

Fruit, yoghurt or cheese and biscuits with sliced and diced salad vegetables and fruit

Drink of water, or well-diluted juice

2.30–3pm   Drink of water or well-diluted juice
Fresh or dried fruit or rice cake, breadstick or savoury biscuit

5–5.30pm   In addition to thick soups, mini sandwiches and the pasta and vegetable dishes your child has been having, try to introduce a variety of different, easy-to-cook meals so that teatime does not become repetitive. Some things you could try are:

Broccoli quiche with salad and homemade French fries

Pizza potatoes with steamed mixed vegetables

Vegetable couscous

Mushroom risotto

Macaroni cheese

Spanish omelette with sautéed potatoes

Fresh fruit

Yoghurt

Cheese and biscuits

Drink of milk, water or well-diluted juice

6.30–7.30pm Drink of milk

Gina Ford's Feeding Plan: 3–6 years

During a child's third year, he should be introduced to using a knife, fork and spoon. This will encourage the development of good table manners and demonstrate how 'grown-up' he is becoming. It is worth buying some sets of inexpensive children's cutlery as smaller sizes are easier to use. Most department stores and supermarkets sell these sets and it is worth involving your child in the choice to encourage an interest in learning to use them.

A child of three should also be encouraged to eat nicely. Praise him for keeping his elbows off the table, sitting sensibly and remembering to say please and thank you. Try to dissuade him from using his fingers at any meals except those that are made up of finger food. If you persevere with this strategy, it reduces mess, sticky hands and accidents.

It is also important for your child to graduate to drinking themselves from normal cups with handles during his third year. Although there will inevitably be the occasional accident and spillage, it is appropriate for him to learn how to coordinate picking up a cup and sipping from it. Some of the children's catalogues sell plastic drinking cups that withstand being dropped. Alternatively, department stores and supermarkets sell tough plastic cups. If your child is particularly clumsy and spillages are all too frequent, try using drinking straws, which can be purchased in bulk. Not only do children love to drink with these, but there is less chance of drips.

From four years of age it is a good idea to purchase some inexpensive crockery, such as side plates. Plain china side plates can cost as little as 99p and are cheaper than plastic novelty plates, do not discolour in the dishwasher and can be replaced if broken. It is important that a child's first experience of using china crockery is not at school.

Most children will refuse to wear a bib by their third year. If your child does not protest, it is certainly worth continuing to use a cloth or plastic bib to save clothes from being soiled. If he does protest, it is understandable, since you are encouraging him to demonstrate grown-up table manners yet grown-ups rarely wear bibs. The best you can hope for is that as your child's table manners improve, the drips and spills will diminish.

Another common challenge with this age group is an older child's tendency to climb down from the table before the meal has finished. This is most likely to happen if the child is sitting on an adult chair. He might be experiencing the freedom of being out of a high chair or harness during the third year, and this can lead to problems. Since adult chairs are not awfully comfortable for children and they can get down all too easily, I would encourage buying either a booster seat or a chair specially designed for children aged 3–6. These can be expensive but can make a big difference to a child's behaviour at mealtimes, and can often be converted into a normal chair when no longer needed. You will need to be firm if he does continue to get down from the table. Praise good behaviour and make it clear to your child that if he does leave the table before you feel that the meal is finished, he cannot come back to request a pudding. Be firm and consistent. Once good practice is established, it will become second nature to sit at the table until he asks to get down and you agree.

Children learn so much by example that it is essential to make time for family meals. Eating at the table with your child is enormously helpful both in terms of mealtime enjoyment and also in emphasising appropriate table manners. A child is much more likely to try a food if he sees you eating it with enjoyment. Plenty of encouragement and praise are the most effective incentives for a child to eat well.

As your child gets older, there are more opportunities for him to be offered food that he has not tried before. These might be in a social context or at school. Do encourage your child to try new foods, with the promise that he does not have to eat them all. Children will often surprise themselves and you by enjoying a more varied diet. One way to encourage variety is to involve them in the food preparation. A child of three will love helping you in the kitchen. Involvement with selecting and cooking a meal will often lead to your child being prepared to try something that he has previously refused.

From the age of three, children often want to recognise the food they are eating, and I have found that they can become very suspicious about stews, pies and casseroles that are not instantly recognisable. Do persevere with new foods since, with encouragement, a child will often be persuaded to eat a little, and gradually you can increase the size of the portion.

Many children begin their first experience of nursery in the run-up to their third birthday. It is essential that your child has eaten a good meal before going to nursery school, since he will use up more energy and have few opportunities for a nutritious snack once there. A well-fed child will concentrate more keenly if sent with a full stomach. A good breakfast is essential for ensuring that your child has the stamina to cope with the added demands of the nursery day. Do allow plenty of time for breakfast. Preparing for morning pre-school or nursery can often be hectic, and it pays off to allow more time for breakfast since a child can rarely be encouraged to eat fast. If your child has tea at a day nursery earlier than is ideal, you might find it is worth asking the staff to give him a smaller meal at 4pm, so that you can give him a small second meal when he gets home. Otherwise you risk your child going to bed at 7pm, having had his last substantial meal at 4pm. This can lead to early disturbed sleep and waking.

If you need to provide a packed lunch for either nursery or school lunchtimes, it is possible to make these just as nutritious as the meals at home. Supermarkets are much better at selling nutritious snacks than they used to be. Try to encourage your child to have a wholemeal sandwich with a protein filling – cheese or ham are the most popular. It's easy to include raw vegetables, cut-up carrot sticks, or cucumber batons. A piece of apple, a banana or a tangerine can be included for the fruit portion. If your child prefers a non-protein filling in his sandwich, such as Marmite or cucumber, supplement the protein with some cooked sausages. Boxes of raisins or dried fruit also make a healthy and tasty addition to a lunch box.

At the end of a morning at nursery or at the end of the school day a child will often be hungry and tired. Try to avoid giving non-nutritious snacks, since these ruin a child's appetite for his proper meal. Instead respond to a hungry child by being organised with mealtimes and having food prepared in advance to quickly appease hunger pangs.

It is less easy to be in control of your child's eating habits if he is enjoying the independence of teas at his friends' houses and the occasional birthday party. Provided he understands that the food often given to children at a party is for special occasions and not to be eaten at home, he will be able to enjoy the odd bit of 'convenience' food, such as crisps and biscuits, without complications. If you are organising a party and would like to offer traditional party food, do remember to offer the children the savoury food, with the good nutritional content, first. If they have eaten some healthy meat or cheese sandwiches and vegetable snacks, most mothers will feel quite relaxed about the appearance of crisps and birthday cake. Unfortunately, once a child of three has seen the less healthy food, it's unlikely he will eat anything nutritious at all.

You might also find that your child will begin to eat less protein during the ages of 3–6. Some children prefer to have two small meals of protein portions, which can be divided between the lunchtime and teatime meals. I have found some of the most popular small protein meals are tuna risotto, home-made chicken nuggets and macaroni cheese.

Although recent government reports indicate that

children of 3–6 are not eating an appropriate amount
of vegetables, I have found that, provided vegetables
are nicely cooked and presented, children love them.
Choose baby vegetables if you can, such as petit
pois, mini carrots, baby sweetcorn, sugarsnaps and
mangetout. These are the most naturally sweet and
tasty. No one enjoys hard, tasteless peas or over-
cooked broccoli. Small salads with crunchy iceberg
lettuce, cucumber chunks, raw carrot and mini tomatoes are also very popular with children, provided
they are not constantly told how good these things
are for them.

Organic Food

Organic foods are produced in traditional ways that restrict the use
of pesticides and other chemicals. Organic food is promoted as
having a higher nutritional value than food produced by modern
farming methods. In fact, opinion is still mixed as to whether this
is true. Shoppers, particularly parents, are faced with a dilemma:
are they failing their families by not buying organic?

The real incentive for parents to buy organic produce is that no
one yet knows the long-term effects of ingesting the chemicals used
on fruit and vegetables. While children are growing rapidly,
repeated exposure to pesticides could be potentially harmful, but
there is as yet no firm evidence.

Buying organic is a personal choice. The important thing is to
make sure your child eats healthy and widely from all the major
food groups, in short, that he has a balanced diet.

Our advice is to ask your supermarket or food retailer about
the produce that is on sale, whether it be organic or not. It's your
right to ask 'how long has it been on sale?' 'How has it been

stored?'; 'Has it been frozen at any point?' Then make your buying decision. It is always best to wash fruit and vegetables prior to eating.

Genetically Modified Food

Genetic modification (GM) involves manipulating the genes of plants to produce particular qualities in them. For example, one plant's resistance to extremely cold temperatures could be passed on to a more tender species to make it resistant too. The idea is that plants can be produced to grow in any conditions.

While many argue that this has to be a good idea – perhaps helping to solve famine in poor parts of the world – others argue that the gene swaps could never occur naturally, so it must be bad. This has led to much heated debate about whether GM food is safe or not. Those for it say that GM crops have been tested more thoroughly than non-GM ones, and that many millions of people and animals eat GM crops with no reported ill effects. Those against say that the long-term safety of GM foods is unknown and that many people are too worried about this to eat them.

While the argument continues to rage, the EU has introduced strict rules about labelling foods that contain GM products. If a food contains genetically modified material or protein, this must be indicated on the label. Similarly, eating places that sell food or drink containing genetically modified material or protein must display a notice indicating this.

Ultimately, we all need to make our own decisions about whether to eat GM foods or not, and if you prefer not to, at least strict labelling will allow you to choose items that are GM-free.

Fluid

While it is important to ensure your child drinks adequately, many parents worry unnecessarily that their children are not taking enough fluid. Below is a simple table for you to check if your child is drinking enough each day. Remember that it shows approximate amounts and that these will vary from day to day. As long as your child is drinking regularly throughout the day, he is more than likely to be getting enough fluid. If a child cannot manage the volumes listed below, he will probably be fine nonetheless, but take care to guard against dehydration in hot weather, and when your child has a temperature or has done lots of exercise. As a rule of thumb, children should have 6–8 drinks a day, with the volume depending on their age.

Remember, it is not just water that counts as fluid. Milk, squash and fruit juice are all mostly fluid, as are purées, soups, mousses, ice cream and jelly. Fruit and vegetables also contain water, and therefore contribute to child's daily fluid intake too.

Babies do not need any fluid other than breast milk, but if it is very hot and your baby is bottle-feeding and has been sweating, you can offer some cooled, boiled water to top him up. Children should be offered fluids throughout the day. They don't tend to drink large amounts at any one time, but will take frequent sips. Offer your child drinks with meals and at least once between meals, and at additional times if he is being very energetic or playing sport. If your child's urine is clear or light in colour, it means he is well hydrated. If his urine is dark and he is not drinking much, keep an eye on him and offer more regular drinks.

Daily fluid requirements from birth to six years

Age	Approximate weight	Fluid intake
0–3 months	5kg (11lb)	750ml (1⅓ pints)
4–6 months	7kg (1st 1lb)	900ml (1½ pints)
7–11 months	9kg (1st 4lb)	1 litre (1¾ pints)
1–3 years	11kg (1st 10lb)	1.1 litres (2 pints)
4–6 years	15kg (2st 5lb)	1.4 litres (2½ pints)

Signs of dehydration

- Dark urine
- Infrequent urination
- Dry mouth, lips and tongue
- Irritable behaviour and sudden worsening of mood
- Weak-sounding cry

Excessive thirst and frequent urination can be a sign of diabetes. If your child is constantly thirsty and asking for drinks all the time, contact your GP immediately.

Watch out that excessive drinking doesn't lead to a poor intake of food. Toddlers who fill up on cow's milk and don't eat much can develop iron deficiency anaemia (see page 164). Similarly, sugary drinks and fruit juice given close to mealtimes can take the edge off your child's appetite for food. Offer water between meals, and only a small amount of water or dilute fruit juice with meals themselves. Once the meal is finished, you can allow your child to quench his thirst with an appropriate drink.

Benjamin, aged 23 months

Problem: Food refusal

Causes: Demand feeding and excessive fluid intake from dependence on a bottle

Benjamin was breast-fed on demand until he was nearly 15 months old. He had always been a poor feeder, looking for a breast-feed every two hours, even after he was weaned onto solids. There was very little food that he enjoyed as a baby, apart from baby rice or rusks mixed with fruit purée or baby fromage frais. During his first year his mother, Catherine, spent hours in the kitchen preparing and cooking different meals to try and expand on the foods that he would eat. Occasionally, Benjamin would take a liking to a new recipe for a few days, but the interest never lasted longer than this and his mother would always resort to giving him a breast-feed or fromage frais when he started to get upset about a certain food.

When Benjamin reached one year Catherine decided to get tough about breast-feeding on demand, and, over a period of two weeks, she gradually increased the length of time between breast-feeds and replaced them with a bottle of formula. While he still continued to be fussy about solids, Benjamin's eating during the day did improve slightly, and Catherine managed to get him off the two middle-of-the-night feeds following advice given in Dr Richard Ferber's book *Solve Your Child's Sleep Problems*. He would still wake up one or twice in the night and would be given a drink from a bottle of well-diluted fruit juice.

Benjamin was drinking, at his various wakings during the night, at least 240ml (8oz) of juice.

When Benjamin was 14 months old Catherine discovered she was pregnant. On the recommendation of a friend she bought my first book, and decided not to breast-feed the second baby during the night. She read the book several times during the pregnancy, and implemented the routines to the letter from the minute her daughter was born. Isabella was a very easy baby, and by five months was sleeping a good 11–12 hour stretch at night. When solids were introduced she took to them really well, and by seven months was eating three good meals a day from a wide variety of the different food groups. While she continued to have two breast-feeds a day, she was happy to take the rest of her milk and fluids from a cup.

This became embarrassing for Catherine as Benjamin, who was now nearly 28 months old, was still having all his milk and fluids from a bottle. His diet was also still very limited. Apart from sausages and ham, he refused all other forms of protein. He would hardly touch breakfast, apart from a small yoghurt, because he was still full from the fluid he had been drinking during the night. He would eat vegetables but only in soup, and his lunch and tea were nearly always the same thing. Lunch was generally a tin of soup with a Marmite or jam sandwich, accompanied by a packet of crisps. Tea would consist of sausages or processed ham and cheese spread or baked beans with sausages on white toast. The soup, crisps and processed meals he ate were of the high-salt convenience variety which were making him thirsty. After all of his meals Benjamin always ate two pots of fromage frais, and during his meals and in between times the only thing that he would drink from a cup was diluted blackcurrant cordial. He also continued to have a full 240ml (8oz) bottle of milk when he first woke in the morning and another at bedtime.

With Isabella now eating solids, Catherine found that she had to prepare two totally different meals for her children. While she had long since accepted that Benjamin would probably always be a poor eater, she was very concerned that as Isabella got older, she didn't begin to be influenced by her brother's poor eating habits. Catherine feared that she might start to refuse the healthy food that she was so happy to take and start demanding the type of food that Benjamin was eating. This concern led her to ring me for advice on how best she could combine both children's meals so that they were eating at the same times, but avoid Isabella being influenced by her older brother's bad eating habits.

I asked Catherine to keep a detailed diary of the times both children ate and drank, what they consumed at these times and the exact amounts. When I received details of what both children had consumed over a three-day period, it was obvious that Isabella was eating a very healthy and varied diet for her age. But Benjamin's diary showed that the type of food he ate was indeed very limited and was eaten in very small amounts. His diary also showed that his two milk feeds morning and night, plus the juice he consumed during the night, came to a daily total of around 840ml (28oz). This amount did not include drinks that he had at mealtimes and in between.

When I questioned Catherine she was not sure of the exact amounts. She would fill the bottle up in the morning and keep topping it up during the day whenever it got near the bottom. Benjamin had access to this bottle at all times. When I asked why she did not keep a closer eye on the amount he was drinking, she explained that she had read a report that many children were becoming dehydrated because they were not getting the recommended 1.2 litres (2 pints) of fluid a day. She assumed the best way to avoid this problem was to allow Benjamin to have access to a drink whenever he felt he was thirsty.

I explained to her that while it was very important for babies and young children to receive enough fluids, children of Benjamin's age cannot comprehend the difference between thirst and hunger, and will often satisfy their hunger needs by drinking fluid. I was fairly sure that part of the reason for Benjamin's fussy feeding was excessive fluid intake. To establish whether this could be the case, I advised Catherine to continue to allow him to drink as usual for the next two days, but this time she should check his bottle every hour, record the amount he had drunk, then pour away the remainder and refill the bottle. This way we would have an accurate idea of what he drank during the day. Two days later Catherine sent me the details and it was much worse than I had envisaged. Between 9am and 5pm, excluding milk feeds and middle-of-the-night diluted juice, Catherine calculated that Benjamin was drinking a whopping 1050ml (35oz) of fluid a day on top of the 840ml (28oz) of milk and middle-of-the-night diluted fruit juice. This was a total of 1900ml (63oz) of fluid a day. It was certainly one of the worst cases of fluid excess that I had heard of, and even Catherine was shocked by the huge amount.

I advised her that in order to improve Benjamin's appetite we should get his total daily intake to a maximum of 1200ml (40oz) a day consumed between 6/7am and 7/8pm. She agreed to this, but with Christmas just 10 days away, she was very hesitant about abandoning his middle-of-the-night drinks, as she was concerned about him screaming in the night for a drink and waking up the family visitors. I suggested that we concentrate on reducing Benjamin's daytime fluids over the Christmas period, and hoped that would see an improvement in his eating so that we could get tough about eliminating night-time fluids after Christmas.

I advised Catherine to continue to allow Benjamin to have his milk and middle-of-the-night fluids from his bottle so that neither she nor he got overly stressed, but that she had to be tough with him about all other fluids. He could still have a drink when he wanted but it must be from a cup, not the bottle. Over the next three days Catherine recorded a slight decrease in the amount that Benjamin was drinking, but he was still consuming nearly 900ml (30oz) a day, in addition to his two milk feeds and middle-of-the-night diluted juice. However, after a lot of fussing and protesting about not being allowed his bottle during the day, he was reluctantly accepting this fluid amount from a cup.

By this time one set of grandparents had arrived for their Christmas visit, so I suggested to Catherine that she enlist their help in occupying Benjamin during the day so that he did not always have access to a cup full of fluids. She should set certain times of the day when he was offered a drink, and if he had not had a drink within 30 minutes of being offered it, the cup should be removed. If an hour later he asked for a drink, he should be offered a piece of fruit instead. This would encourage his appetite and also satisfy some of his daily fluid requirements. Benjamin's grandparents ensured that he was taken out to plenty of activities in the morning and the afternoon, but only one 180ml (6oz) cup of diluted juice was allowed, which had to be offered between 9am and no later than 10.30am, and around 2pm and no later than 3.30pm. He could also be offered a similar amount of fluid at mealtimes, but only after he had eaten at least half his solids. In addition, over three days we gradually reduced his morning bottle of milk to 180ml (6oz).

Within five days, Benjamin's excessive daytime fluid had been dramatically reduced. He was having 180ml (6oz) of milk in the morning when he awoke. At lunch and teatime he would drink 90–150ml (3–5oz), and in between meals he would drink 90–120ml (3–4oz). This huge reduction in his daily fluid intake had an excellent effect on his eating, and although he still continued to be fussy about the types of foods he ate, the amounts he consumed increased dramatically, which meant that he cut his bedtime milk feed down to 210ml (7oz). His daily intake of fluids between 7am and 7.30pm was now 720–810ml (24–27oz), and because his eating had improved so much during the day, he was drinking less in the night.

Once Christmas was over, we agreed to resolve the problem of Benjamin still drinking his milk from a bottle both night and morning, and still needing a drink of diluted juice to settle himself back to sleep in the middle of the night. I suggested that we begin by reducing the amount of juice that was given in the middle of the night. Catherine should, over the next four nights, reduce the amount in each bottle by 30ml (1oz), and gradually dilute it more and more until she was putting only water in the bottle. I explained that she must be prepared for several unsettled nights once he was being offered only water during the night. She could go in and reassure him every 10 minutes should he get very upset, but she was not to lift him out of the cot or resort to settling him with juice. The first two nights were very difficult for Catherine, as she was in and out of his room several times between 2am and 6am, but she did not relent, and on the third night she managed to settle him back to sleep without offering him a drink.

On the fourth night I suggested that we offer Benjamin only one drink, but in a cup instead of a bottle. That night was a particularly bad one, and Catherine decided that she was ready to abandon the cup of water altogether and use controlled crying in order to get him back to sleep. She then had a further three very difficult nights of sleep training but on the fourth night Benjamin slept through until nearly 6am. On my advice, she abandoned the morning bottle of milk and replaced it with a cup of milk. The first few mornings Benjamin fussed and protested but Catherine persevered and, by the end of the week, he happily drank 180ml (6oz) of milk from a cup. We then replaced his bedtime milk feed from the bottle with a cup, so he was now taking all his fluids from a cup. Because he was no longer drinking during the night, he did increase the amount of fluid he had during the day, but we ensured that he was offered only water mid-way between meals so that it did not interfere with his appetite. He was now drinking 440–530ml (15–18oz) of fluid between his morning and bedtime feed, and a drink at teatime. At lunchtime he would drink 90–120ml (3–4oz) and his drinks of water between meals were usually 150–180ml (5–6oz). His daily fluid intake was now 960–1020ml (32–34oz), and he was eating very substantial amounts at all his meals. Catherine was a bit worried that he was now below the daily fluid recommendations, and for several days increased the amount of fluid he was having. However, she noticed that he immediately became very fussy about his meals, particularly his tea. I advised her that 960–1020ml (32–34oz) of fluid a day, along with a good intake of fruit and vegetables daily, was more than sufficient. Benjamin did continue to be very limited in his range of foods, but I reassured Catherine that as long as he was getting a selection of foods from all the food groups, she should not pressure him too much to try lots of different things. It would be better to establish several weeks of him getting used to happily eating good amounts, then gradually try to expand on the range of foods. Now that he was happy to eat some of the same types of food as Isabella, Catherine and I devised a meal plan that enabled her to cook food that was suitable for both children and at the same meal. Eating with his sister then encouraged Benjamin to become more adventurous with his food and to expand on the different meals that he would eat, but Catherine had to continue being extra vigilant about the amount of fluid he was given, as the days on which she was more relaxed and allowed him to drink excessively he would be much fussier about eating. I advised Catherine that she should fill two bottles each morning – one with water and one with well-diluted juice – with the exact amount he was allowed to drink that day. This would make it easier for her to monitor his fluid intake.

Benjamin's situation really stemmed from being breast-fed on demand long after solids were introduced, and being allowed to drink fluids from a bottle after the age of one year. Toddlers of this age can drink fluid much more quickly from a bottle than a cup and when their fluid intake

Gina Ford's Top Tip

Encourage your toddler to eat at least half his meal before having a drink, then teach him to put his cup down in between sips. This will prevent him from drinking too much fluid too quickly and taking the edge off his appetite.

is not structured to fit in with mealtimes it can result in them confusing hunger with thirst.

Healthy drinks

Finding a healthy drink on the shelves of supermarkets can be a very difficult task. There are rows and rows of enticing bottles in many tempting flavours and bright colours, and children are drawn to the familiar brands advertised on television. Schools, meanwhile, have vending machines full of drinks that children love but parents worry about. The soft drinks industry is a multi-million pound business, but the sad fact is that most of the drinks it produces can be quite harmful to children. They contain high amounts of sugar, which can rot teeth and lead to excess weight and even obesity. Some of them also contain additives, colourings and caffeine, which can cause hyperactivity and behavioural problems.

Artificially sweetened drinks

If sugary drinks are bad for children, presumably sugar-free ones are better? Well, yes and no. All drinks advertised as sugar-free contain artificial sweeteners, but experts recommend treating these with caution. The Food Standards Agency, for example, as a precautionary measure, advises parents to give young children aged 1–4 years no more than three cups a day of dilutable soft drinks containing the artificial sweetener cyclamate.

Did you know?

There are, on average, 12 teaspoons of sugar in a can of soft drink, and even more in a bottle of 'sports drink'. Some fruit-flavoured drinks contain only 5 per cent fruit juice, but up to 17 teaspoons of sugar in one bottle.

An alarming 20 per cent of British children aged 7–10 drink nearly 10 cans of soft drink per week.

Paul Sacher's Top Tips for Healthier Drinks

- Offer one cup (150ml/5oz) per day of pure fruit juice instead of squash or fizzy drinks. Although all these drinks contain sugar, which can lead to excessive weight gain and contribute to dental caries, pure fruit juice also contains useful nutrients, such as vitamin C.
- Make your child smoothies by blending fruit on its own, or adding some milk.
- If your child has to have fruit juice, offer it at mealtimes. The sugar is absorbed more slowly with food and will not lead to a blood-sugar high that might cause excessive energy, followed by a blood-sugar low that creates a craving for more high-energy foods. A small amount of fruit juice with meals also helps the iron in food to be absorbed because it contains vitamin C.
- Drinks given in bottles cause increased dental decay. Try to wean your baby off the bottle by introducing a cup at six months. Do not allow your child to go to bed with a bottle, as this is associated with high levels of dental caries and there is also a risk of choking.
- Limit your child to 150ml (5oz) of pure fruit juice per day. This keeps down his sugar intake and counts (only once a day) as one portion of the recommended five daily portions of fruit and vegetables.
- Offer water or milk rather than sugary drinks. If children insist on fruit juice, dilute it with water (1:5) to make it less sugary (and last longer).
- Get your child to brush his teeth after a sugary drink.
- Children like drinking out of trendy sports-type bottles, so try filling them from the tap.

Q How can I tell which drinks contain cyclamate and how can I make sure my child does not exceed the safe limit?

A Products containing cyclamates are required by law to be labelled 'with sweetener' or 'with sugar and sweeteners', and include the names cyclamate, cyclamic acid or E952 in the list of ingredients. Always read the labels.

When preparing dilutable soft drinks containing cyclamate, dilute them more for children than you would for an adult.

Do not give children more than three cups a day (about 180ml/6oz each) of drinks containing cyclamate.

Other artificial sweeteners

Young children drinking large amounts of dilutable soft drinks containing aspartame, acesulfame K or saccharin would not exceed the safe limit for these sweeteners, but it is probably wiser not to allow excessive amounts of drinks containing any artificial sweetener. At the very least, they will create a sweet tooth in your child, which can be a hard taste to break.

Caffeine

Caffeine is a stimulant found naturally in certain foods and drinks, such as chocolate, tea and coffee, but is also added to some items, such as cola and sports drinks, to give an energy boost. However, caffeine is addictive, and gradually more and more may be required to produce the same effect. While adults might feel they need or enjoy the 'lift' provided by caffeine, children are more likely to be adversely affected by it. For example, caffeine is passed through breast milk, so it might make your baby difficult to settle. In this case, try eliminating caffeine from your diet and see if there is any improvement. (Note that you might experience headaches, lethargy and various other withdrawal symptoms.) In older children, restless and fretful behaviour can often be traced back to the caffeine in drink or food.

We recommend that you avoid giving children all drinks containing caffeine. Why would you give an addictive substance to a child?

Summary of drinks for children

Age	Suitable main drink
0–12 months	Breast milk, formula or water
1–2 years	Breast milk, follow-on formula and/or full-fat cow's milk
2–4 years	Full-fat or semi-skimmed milk (also known as low-fat milk)
5–6 years	Full-fat, semi-skimmed or skimmed milk (also known as fat-free milk)

Note: Always dilute pure fruit juice for under ones but pure fruit juice can be given undiluted for the over ones. Squashes, cordials and other such drinks that require diluting should not be given to under ones but can be given to over ones. However, always make them up according to manufacturer's instructions.

Assessing Growth

Many parents have been in the situation where someone has commented on the size or shape of their child. 'What a big boy he is!' or 'She must feed very well, judging by the size of her!' and 'Are you sure you're feeding her enough? She looks very small for her age.' Comments like this can be very distressing to a parent and often cause unnecessary anxiety. So how do you tell if your child is growing appropriately?

There are many factors that influence a child's growth, some of them modifiable and others simply hereditary. All children are born with a genetic blueprint, inherited from both parents, that determines how they will grow. If both Mum and Dad's families are short, it is highly unlikely that the child will be tall. If one parent is tall and the other short, it is a bit of a gamble as to how the child will turn out. The environment also plays an important part in growth, but the future is largely dependent upon the genetic blueprint.

So where does nutrition fit in? Well, a child can be designed to be really tall, but if he has insufficient nutrition during childhood, he is unlikely to meet that genetic potential. An extreme example is found in children from developing countries who, after prolonged periods of poor diet and insufficient intakes of vital nutrients, are often stunted in growth. Apart from genetics, which we can't change, a good diet is paramount in ensuring that your child grows as best he can.

Simply observing children to determine how well they are growing is far from reliable. Even the most experienced health professionals cannot tell how good a child's growth is just by looking at him. This is where the child health care record, or 'red book' as it is known, comes in. All children in the UK are given this book when they are born, which is used to keep a record of important dates, such as immunisations and health checks, but it also contains a section of growth charts. These are graphs with lots of lines called centiles (or percentiles) that represent percentages of the population.

When you take your child to your local clinic, the health visitor will measure and weigh him, then record the results on the growth chart. Where a child falls on the growth charts at birth is largely pre-determined by the size of the mother and genetics; how he grows from then onwards is a combination of genes and nutrition. Children should follow roughly the same line, and any major deviations should be cause for concern. If the weight drops by two lines or centiles, this is classified as 'faltering growth' (see page 183) and should be dealt with by a qualified health professional. Note the following guidelines:

- Always make sure that your child is weighed and measured at the appropriate times.

- Make sure he is undressed appropriately for the measurements, i.e. naked if a baby, in underwear if older.

- If your child is growing roughly along the same line of the chart, you don't need to be concerned about his growth.

- If your child starts to cross the lines upwards, seek professional advice (see page vi), as this may be the start of him becoming overweight.

• If your child starts to cross lines downwards, this is a sign of poor growth, which may be due to factors such as illness or inadequate diet, so seek professional advice (see page 201).

Remember that the growth charts are based on data collected from a large sample of British children, so they are representative of all children in the UK.

Birth weight facts
• Average birth weight for babies in the United Kingdom is between 3.15kg (7lb 5oz) and 3.3kg (7lb 11oz) for both sexes.
• Some weight loss during the first 5-7 days is normal while feeding is established.
• Birth weight is normally regained by the 10th–14th day of life.

Average weight gain for the first year
• 200g (7oz) per week for the first three months
• 150g (5oz) per week for the second three months
• 100g (3½oz) per week for the third three months
• 50–75g (1¾–2½oz) per week for the fourth three months

Q How often should my child be weighed and measured?

A All babies are weighed at birth. Thereafter, babies who are growing normally should be weighed only at immunisation and when there is contact with a health professional, such as health visitor or GP.

   Babies under the age of six months should not be weighed more than once every two weeks. From six months to two years they may be weighed once a month if there is a need.

Length should be measured every six months and when there is concern about a baby or toddler's growth or weight gain.

Children over two years of age should be weighed and have their height measured at entry to school. Do not weigh children too frequently or you might instil anxiety, which could lead to problems later in life.

The table opposite, divided into different centiles – 2nd, 50th and 98th – can be used as an indication of your child's weight status. Remember this table takes only weight into account and is an average for children in the UK. Some children will be very heavy and tall, while others may be short and therefore have a low weight. If you are concerned, ask your health visitor, practice nurse or GP to assess your child on a growth chart.

Did you know?

At the end of the first year of life, a baby reaches almost half its final adult height. The average gain in length during the first year is 25cm (10in). During the second year, the average toddler will gain 2.5kg (5lb 8oz) in weight and a further 12cm (4½in) in length. Thereafter, young children continue to gain approximately 2kg (4lb 6oz) per year and 10cm (4in) in length, which gradually declines to 6cm (2½in) per year, until they reach their growth spurt at puberty.

Where does your child's weight fall?

If your child falls on the 2nd centile, he is among 2 per cent of children of that weight at that age; 98 per cent of his contemporaries in the UK weigh more than he does. Children who fall below the 2nd

Weight chart for children aged 0–6½ years

Age	Males			Females		
Centiles	2nd	50th	98th	2nd	50th	98th
0 months	2.7kg	3.6kg	4.7kg	2.6kg	3.4kg	4.3kg
	(6lb)	(8lb)	(10lb)	(6lb)	(7lb)	(9lb)
3 months	4.9kg	6.3kg	7.8kg	4.7kg	5.7kg	7.3kg
	(11lb)	(1st)	(1st 3lb)	(10lb)	(13lb)	(1st 2lb)
6 months	6.5kg	8.1kg	9.9kg	6.2kg	7.5kg	9.3kg
	(1st)	(1st 4lb)	(1st 8lb)	(1st)	(1st 2lb)	(1st 6lb)
9 months	7.4kg	9.2kg	11.4kg	7.0kg	8.6kg	10.6kg
	(1st 2lb)	(1st 6lb)	(1st 11lb)	(1st 1lb)	(1st 5lb)	(1st 9lb)
12 months	8.2kg	10.2kg	12.5kg	7.7kg	9.5kg	11.7kg
	(1st 4lb)	(1st 8lb)	(1st 13lb)	(1st 3lb)	(1st 7lb)	(1st 12lb)
1½ years	9.3kg	11.4kg	14.2kg	8.8kg	10.8kg	13.5kg
	(1st 6lb)	(1st 11lb)	(2st 3lb)	(1st 5lb)	(1st 10lb)	(2st 2lb)
2.0 years	10.1kg	12.5kg	15.6kg	9.7kg	12.0kg	15.0kg
	(1st 8lb)	(1st 13lb)	(2st 6lb)	(1st 7lb)	(1st 12lb)	(2st 5lb)
2½ years	10.9kg	13.5kg	17.0kg	10.5kg	13.0kg	17.0kg
	(1st 10lb)	(2st 2lb)	(2st 9lb)	(1st 9lb)	(2st 1lb)	(2st 9lb)
3.0 years	11.8kg	14.7kg	18.5kg	11.3kg	14.0kg	18.2kg
	(1st 12lb)	(2st 4lb)	(2st 13lb)	(1st 11lb)	(2st 3lb)	(2st 12lb)
3½ years	12.6kg	15.6kg	19.8kg	12.0kg	15.0kg	19.5kg
	(2st)	(2st 6lb)	(3st 2lb)	(1st 12lb)	(2st 5lb)	(3st 1lb)
4.0 years	13.3kg	16.5kg	21.1kg	13.0kg	16.0kg	21.5kg
	(2st 1lb)	(2st 8lb)	(3st 4lb)	(2st 1lb)	(2st 7lb)	(3st 5lb)
4½ years	14.0kg	17.5kg	22.5kg	13.5kg	17.0kg	23.0kg
	(2st 3lb)	(2st 10lb)	(3st 7lb)	(2st 2lb)	(2st 9lb)	(3st 9lb)
5.0 years	14.8kg	18.6kg	24.2kg	14.0kg	18.0kg	24.5kg
	(2st 5lb)	(2st 13lb)	(3st 11lb)	(2st 3lb)	(2st 12lb)	(3st 12lb)
5½ years	15.8kg	20.0kg	26.0kg	15.0kg	19.4kg	26.5kg
	(2st 7lb)	(3st 2lb)	(4st 1lb)	(2st 5lb)	(3st 1lb)	(4st 2lb)
6½ years	17.4kg	22.0kg	29.5kg	16.5kg	21.5kg	30.0kg
	(2st 10lb)	(2st 6lb)	(4st 9lb)	(2st 8lb)	(3st 5lb)	(4st 10lb)

Source: *Nutritional Requirements for Children in Health and Disease*, Great Ormond Street Hospital for Children NHS Trust. Produced by the Dietetic Department, 3rd edition, September 2000.

centile are considered underweight. While your child may be perfectly healthy, ask your GP to check that there is no underlying problem (see page 183).

If your child falls on the 50th centile, he is of average weight for his age. In fact, any weight between the 2nd and the 98th centiles is considered normal. However, have him measured to make sure his height is appropriate to his weight. For example, if his weight is on the 50th centile, while his length is just above the 2nd centile, this means that his weight is a lot higher than it should be for his height.

If your child falls above the 98th centile for weight, he will be among 2 per cent of children of that height, at that age and probably come from a family with members who are large, perhaps muscly or 'big boned'. Have his height measured to confirm this. If it is far below the 98th centile, he may be classified as overweight, which means that his weight will negatively affect his health (see page 179), perhaps causing asthma or problems with joints.

It is important not to make a big issue of weight. Remember that children learn by example, so if you weigh yourself or your child every day, then you are likely to impart the message that weight is a source of anxiety. We are all different shapes and sizes, and weight alone is not a complete indictor of health; the ratio of muscle to fat is also important, but cannot be determined by stepping on the scales. Always encourage a healthy diet and regular activity to ensure your children grow to reach their full potential.

2
The First Stages of Life

Pregnancy

Q How much should I eat during pregnancy?

A Eating well is important for everyone, but especially so
   when you are pregnant, and even when you are planning a
   pregnancy. The old idea of 'eating for two' is a myth, and it
   is important to watch your intake to make sure you don't
   gain excessive weight during pregnancy and then struggle
   to return to your previous healthy body weight when the
   baby arrives. You should eat a normal diet right until the
   last trimester (the last 12 weeks), when your requirement
   increases by an extra 200 calories per day. This requirement can be satisfied in various ways:

   • 1 apple and a chicken thigh
   • 1 glass of freshly squeezed orange juice and a hard-boiled egg
   • 1 handful of peanuts
   • 4 small roast potatoes

   A healthy diet during pregnancy will ensure that your
   developing baby has a good blood supply, but it will also

help to maintain your body's nutrient stores and keep you in the best of health to meet the demands of looking after a newborn. Women who, for example, have a poor intake of calcium during pregnancy have a higher risk of weak or brittle bones later in life.

Choose foods from the food groups outlined below, and follow the recommended number of portions to ensure you are getting the right balance of nutrients needed for a healthy diet during pregnancy.

Group One: milk and dairy products
Cow's milk, lassi, yoghurt, fromage frais, cottage cheese and hard cheese.
Choose low-fat alternatives whenever you can, and try to eat 2–3 portions per day. (One portion is equal to a glass of milk or a standard pot of yoghurt or a matchbox-sized piece of cheese. Pregnant women should avoid non-pasteurised cheeses.)

Group Two: carbohydrates or starchy foods
Bread, fortified breakfast cereals, oats, other cereals such as barley and rye, plain and savoury biscuits, potatoes, yams, millet, pasta, semolina and rice.
Eat all types of carbohydrate, and choose wholemeal or high-fibre varieties whenever you can. Increasing the fibre in your diet and drinking at least eight cups of fluid (1.5 litres/2½ pints) per day will help to avoid constipation. Include 5–9 portions from this group per day. (One portion is equal to a slice of bread or a small potato or half a cup of cooked rice, pasta, etc.)

Group Three: vegetables and fruit
Leafy and green vegetables (cabbage, spring greens, kale, cauliflower and broccoli); root vegetables (carrots, swede, turnips); salad vegetables (tomatoes, cucumber), mushrooms, sweetcorn, marrow; fruit and fruit juices.
Eat at least five portions of fruit and vegetables every day when pregnant. Fruit juice counts only once as a portion per day.

Group Four: meat and meat alternatives

Meat, poultry, eggs, fish, lentils, peas, beans, peanuts and soya.
Choose low-fat alternatives whenever you can, and eat 2–3 portions
per day. (One portion is equal to one egg, 100g/3½ oz of fish,
chicken or meat, or 6 tablespoons of cooked lentils, peas or beans.)

Group Five: occasional foods

*Cakes, biscuits, sweetened squash, sweetened desserts, cream, ice
cream, sugar, jam, honey, crisps, savoury snacks, fried and fatty foods.*
Try not to eat these items frequently as they are high in sugar and
fat but offer little else in terms of nutrition. If you must eat them,
have only small amounts.

Supplements

The Department of Health (D.H) recommends supplements of folic
acid and vitamin D during pregnancy.

Folic acid

Folic acid, also called folate or folacin, is vital for healthy blood
cells, forming new body cells, particularly red cells in the blood,
and healthy growth. During pregnancy, it is involved in the forma-
tion of the unborn baby's spinal cord.

Folic acid is found primarily in leafy green vegetables,
oranges, wholemeal bread and fortified cereals. It is easily
destroyed during long storage, and up to 50 per cent can be lost
during cooking.

Eating plenty of foods rich in folic acid during pregnancy can
help reduce the risk of neural tube defects, such as spina bifida.
The D.H advises women planning pregnancy to take an additional
folic acid supplement and to use fortified foods. Start taking a daily
supplement of 400mcg as soon as you stop using contraceptives,
or as soon as you think you may be pregnant. Keep taking the supplement for the first 12 weeks of pregnancy.

Vitamins

The only vitamin supplement women are advised to take during pregnancy is vitamin D, to ensure they get an intake of 10 mcg per day. (The function and sources of vitamin D are discussed on page 35.)

Any further choice of supplements is up to you. If, for example, you don't always eat a balanced diet, or you have suffered with prolonged periods of morning sickness or loss of appetite, your body's stores of vitamins may be depleted, so a supplement can fill the gap. Similarly, strict vegetarians or vegans might like to top up their vitamin B_{12}, as it is found only in animal foods.

Don't go overboard with supplements. For example, taking multivitamins to get your daily folic acid requirement could give you excessive amounts of certain vitamins, which can be dangerous to your developing baby. More is not better.

Iron and calcium are especially important during pregnancy, when requirements are increased, so make sure you get adequate amounts (see pages 36 and 37).

The belief that fish is good for the brain is, it seems, not such an old wives' tale after all. There is good scientific evidence that omega-3 fats, which are found in fish, are important in the development of the foetus and in later stages of life. Oily fish, such as mackerel, herring, salmon, sardine and trout, are a very good source of omega-3 fats, so try to eat at least one portion (100g/3½oz) a week.

Foods to avoid during pregnancy

- Liver or liver products, such as pâté or liver sausage, because they contain excessive amounts of vitamin A.

- Soft cheese, such as Brie and Camembert; uncooked eggs, found in mayonnaise and desserts such as zabaglione; and raw or undercooked meats. All these foods carry the risk of food poisoning.

In addition, take great care with food hygiene. Make sure that cooked foods are kept separate from raw foods, and that clean surfaces and kitchen utensils are used when cooking.

Breast-feeding

We have all heard that breast is best, and there is much evidence that breast-feeding your child will give him the best start in life. Breast milk is packed full of goodness, containing all the nutrients that babies need to grow and develop, and it also contains antibodies that strengthen your child's immune system and help protect against illness. Other factors in it are essential for the development of the brain and for things such as vision. In addition, breast milk helps to keep babies' stools soft and stimulates their bowels to work properly.

Advantages of breast-feeding

Mother	Infant
Inexpensive and convenient	Ideal nutritional composition
Possible health benefits (reduced risk of ovarian cancer, premenopausal breast cancer and osteoporosis)	Protective factors against illness
	Possible psychological benefits

If you are breast-feeding, it is important to have a balanced diet and eat from all the major food groups (see page 72). Make sure you get enough calcium by eating plenty of dairy products, fish containing soft bones, such as canned pilchards and sardines, dark green, leafy vegetables, and pulses, such as beans and lentils. If you do not eat dairy produce, or not in sufficient quantities, make sure you do take a calcium supplement (1200mg per day). Insufficient calcium in your diet will lead to weaker bones later in life.

It is also important to have a good daily intake of vitamin C. Since vitamin C is not stored in the body, it must be obtained every day by eating fruit and vegetables.

The amount of fluid you drink can affect the volume of breast milk you produce, so you will need to drink about 2 litres (3½ pints) per day to avoid getting dehydrated. It's a good idea to make sure you drink a large glass of water, milk or fruit juice every time you sit down to feed the baby. This extra amount is on top of your usual fluid intake and the drinks you have when thirsty. Note that alcohol and caffeine pass into breast milk, so large intakes of both should be avoided during lactation. Highly spicy or strong-tasting foods can also affect the taste of breast milk and may unsettle some babies.

Q **How can I tell if my baby is getting enough breast milk?**

A It is impossible to measure the amount of breast milk a baby drinks when breast-feeding. If the baby is growing appropriately, he is definitely getting enough breast milk. The recommendations (see page 87) are that mothers should breast-feed exclusively for six months to give their babies the best start in life. Solids should be introduced at six months, and as the amount of solids increases, the breast-feeding should be decreased to promote your baby's appetite for food. If your baby is over six months and continually being put on the breast, he is likely to be a poor eater. Try offering solids before milk feeds to encourage your baby to eat.

A healthy breast-fed baby will have the following characteristics:

- Good steady weight gain.
- A good skin colour.
- Be mostly contented, responsive and alert.
- Have frequent wet nappies.
- Produce bright yellow soft stools (the frequency is unimportant).

Q Can the food I eat affect my baby?

A Everything you eat is processed by your body and can be
passed to your baby via breast milk. Certain babies from
families with a history of allergy can react to foods in their
mother's diet, such as cow's milk. It is very important,
however, that any foods avoided are replaced by suitable
alternatives. For example, if you suspect that cow's milk
products may be provoking a reaction in your baby and
you decide to exclude them from your diet while you are
breast-feeding, make sure you replace them with a calcium
supplement and the calories from other foods.

Some people believe that foods eaten by a breast-feeding
mother can cause colic in her baby. If you notice that your
baby is fretful or cries a lot after some breast-feeds, it
might be worth keeping a food diary of everything you eat
and drink so that you can look back after a week or so and
see if there is a common food implicated.

It is known that toxins such as alcohol, caffeine and
nicotine are passed through the breast milk, so it is best to
avoid these while you are breast-feeding.

Bottle-feeding

The bottle can be a useful alternative to the breast as it means that
the baby does not have to be dependent on the mother for its nutrition. Bottle-feeding can also be equally nutritious, especially if
expressed breast milk is used. Failing that, there is a wide variety of
suitable infant formulas to choose from (see page 82).

Expressing

Breast-feeding poses a problem for mothers who are not at home
with their babies all day, so this is where expressing milk comes in.
Expressing can be done by hand or by using a manual or electric

breast pump. Breast milk can be stored in the fridge for up to 24 hours, or frozen for up to one month, then defrosted and used within 24 hours. (Defrost it in a container of room-temperature water, making sure the water remains well below the cap of the bottle to prevent contamination of the milk, then heat it to the optimal temperature for feeding.) Some mothers choose to bottle-feed their babies exclusively on breast milk, while others use a combination of breast milk and formula milk. Apart from the benefits to the baby, expressing will help to keep your milk supply high and enable you to breast-feed for longer. Your GP or health visitor can provide more information.

Polly, aged six months

Problem: Low milk intake

Cause: Introducing formula milk and solids too quickly, which led to a reduction in the mother's milk supply

Polly weighed just over 3.6kg (8lb) at birth; she took to the breast well and regained her birth weight within eight days. She was a very placid, easy baby and fell naturally into a routine of her own accord. By the time she was three weeks, she was settling well at 6.30pm, waking around midnight, feeding well and settling back to sleep until 5.30am. This continued until Polly was nearly six weeks old, when she suddenly started to wake up around 10pm demanding a feed. She would then wake up again around 2am and 5am and refuse to settle back to sleep without a feed. This pattern continued for a further two weeks. Caroline, her mother, was becoming so exhausted getting up twice a night that she decided to follow the advice of friends and introduce a bottle of formula at the 10pm feed to see if it would get Polly back to sleeping longer in the night.

Within a week Polly had started to sleep through to 3am,

and by the time she was 12 weeks she was sleeping through to 7am from her last formula feed at 10pm. By 16 weeks Polly was still sleeping through the night from the 10pm feed, but started demanding to be fed much sooner than usual during the day. With a good weight gain of 200–240g (7–8oz) each week, she was now weighing well over 6.6kg (15lb). Polly was such a good weight and was showing all the typical signs of needing to be weaned that Caroline introduced her to a small amount of baby rice and fruit at four months.

Polly loved the solids and within a week she was having solids twice a day and sleeping through to 6.30am with only a 90ml (3oz) formula feed at 10pm. Caroline decided to drop this feed, as she was sure that Polly could get through the night without it. But, as she was planning to return to work when Polly was six months, Caroline decided to introduce a bottle of formula at the 2pm feed, so Polly continued to take some of her milk from a bottle. She was very reluctant to take this bottle and would never drink more than 90ml (3oz) at this feed. However, her weight gain was still good and she continued to sleep from 7pm to 6.30am, so Caroline was not overly concerned about this. At six months, when Caroline returned to work, she introduced protein at Polly's 11am feed and replaced the breast-feed with a drink of cool, boiled water. Polly was now having a breast-feed at 6.30am and 6.30pm, and a bottle of formula at 2.30pm. Within a week of commencing the new feeding pattern, Polly began waking up at 5am. Caroline attempted to settle her back to sleep by patting her or offering her water, but this rarely worked. Such an early start to the day resulted in Polly being very grumpy and overtired by the time Caroline got home from work at 4pm and wanting to go to sleep at 6pm in the evening.

When I received Polly's feeding chart it was obvious that the reason for her 5am waking was one of genuine hunger caused by the sudden drop in her daily milk intake. I believed that there were two reasons for the reduction in her milk intake. The first was that, unlike most babies, Polly did not automatically increase the amount she drank at the 2.30pm feed when the 11.30am feed was dropped. The second reason was that her mother's milk supply had decreased very rapidly when she started work and went down to two breast-feeds a day. This meant that in addition to the too-small feed at 2.30pm, Polly was not getting enough milk at the 6.30pm feed, resulting in a genuine need to feed at 5am.

Unfortunately, because solid food had been introduced at the same time as the formula feed at 2.30pm the combination filled Polly up so much that it made her less keen to take milk from a bottle at this feed. Introducing a second lot of solids at 5pm, within a week of introducing the first lot of solids, meant that she very quickly cut down on the amount of milk she took from the breast at 6pm, resulting in a 5am waking through a genuine need for a milk feed. Although Caroline's breasts were very full in the morning and Polly did take a good feed at this time, she could not take enough in this one feed to compensate for the big drop at her other two feeds. By the time Polly reached six months, she was having three solid meals a day.

A baby of six months still needs at least three full milk feeds a day, and some may need up to five if they have not been weaned. Milk is still very important at this stage and it is vital that it is not replaced too quickly with solids, which is what happened in Polly's case. The problem was made worse by the fact that she was introduced to formula at the same time as she was quickly put onto two solid meals a day. This also affected the amount of breast milk that Caroline was producing. Having replaced the 2.30pm feed with formula and introduced solids twice a day within such a short time meant that Polly very quickly started to take less and less from the breast, resulting in Caroline's milk supply decreasing very rapidly. She was very keen to breast-feed Polly in the morning and the evening until she was a year old, but was anxious that this was not going to be possible if her milk production kept decreasing as Polly increased her solids.

I explained to Caroline that the first thing we had to do was to boost her milk supply so that Polly did not continue to increase her intake of solids too quickly. Since Caroline was at work from 10am to 4pm, it was not possible to put Polly to the breast more frequently during the day, and expressing at work was not an option. I suggested that she should express in the evening before bedtime and use that milk for Polly's 2.30pm feed in the afternoon. She should then offer her both breasts at 5/5.30pm before offering solids: this would ensure that Polly did not fill up with solids, which were reducing her milk intake too much at bedtime. At 7pm she should then be offered the breast again, before being offered a top-up of formula milk. I advised Caroline to keep following this plan until Polly was taking at least 180ml (6oz) of expressed milk at the 2.30pm feed. Once she was taking this, she could then start to give Polly her solids first at 5pm, as she should have had two-thirds of her daily requirement of milk by this time.

I also advised Caroline to keep a very close watch on the amount of solids she gave Polly at 5pm as it was important that she did not increase them so quickly that the baby refused to take a good milk feed from both breasts at bedtime.

Caroline continued with this feeding pattern for a further two months, at which stage she felt that she could gradually decrease, then cut out the 10pm expressing and reintroduce a formula feed at 2.30pm without it causing a sudden decrease in Polly's morning and evening breast-feed.

This is a very common problem that many mothers who are returning to work find themselves having to deal with. I always advise those who wish to breast-feed for more than four months to include at least one expressing during the day once their baby is weaned onto solids as this helps to maintain a good milk supply, which can otherwise decrease very rapidly once a breast-feeding mother returns to work. I also suggest that when replacing a breast-feed with a formula-feed it is important not to do so at the same time as introducing solids. I believe that the introduction of formula milk and two solid meals a day in such a short period of time severely affected Polly's appetite for her other breast-feeds, quickly reducing the amount of milk that Caroline was producing. Caroline would have been better establishing a full formula-feed at 2.30pm and waiting until Polly went through her next growth spurt before introducing solids, as this would have allowed more time for Polly's digestive system to adjust to the formula, and more time for her to establish full feeds at the remaining two breast-feeds.

Infant formulas

If you decide not to breast-feed, choosing the right infant formula is essential, and things have come a long way since the days of powdered cow's milk. There are many formulas available, some with different nutrients for different ages. Infant formulas are designed to resemble human breast milk as closely as possible, but they lack many of the important factors found in the real thing. Companies are constantly researching to give their products the nutritional edge.

At one time infant formulas were heavily marketed to parents, which led to a decrease in the number of women choosing to breast-feed. As a result, there is now very strict legislation governing the way infant formulas can be marketed to parents. For this reason it can often be difficult to get objective information on which formula to choose.

The two types of formula suitable for the first year of life both contain whey and casein. The choice to be made boils down to selecting the one that most closely resembles breast milk – namely, the one

Examples of first-stage and follow-on formulas

Age	Type of milk	Brand
0–12 months	First stage: whey dominant	Aptamil First (Milupa), Farley's First Milk (Farley), Hipp Organic Infant Milk (Hipp), Infant Formula 1 (Boots), Omneocomfort 1 (Cow & Gate), Premium (Cow & Gate), SMA Gold (SMA Nutrition)
0–12 months	First stage: casein dominant	Aptamil Extra (Milupa), Farley's Second Milk (Farley), Infant Formula 2 (Boots), Milumil (Milupa), Plus (Cow & Gate), SMA White (SMA Nutrition)
6–24 months	Follow-on formulas: all casein dominant	Farley's Follow-on Milk (Farley), Follow-on Milk (Boots), Forward (Milupa), Organic Follow-on Milk (Hipp), Next Steps (Cow & Gate), Omneocomfort 2 (Cow & Gate) Progress (SMA Nutrition), Step Up (Cow & Gate),

Information compiled February 2004. Note that the range and availability of products is subject to change

that contains a higher proportion of whey. Those that contain more casein are generally marketed for the hungrier baby, but the evidence for this is debatable. The best advice is to choose a formula and then stick with it. Changing formulas frequently is not recommended.

Follow-on formulas are available for infants aged 6–24 months and may be beneficial for some. They contain higher levels of protein, calories and certain vitamins, and can offer benefits to babies who do not get much sunlight or have a poor diet. If your baby is weaned properly and eats a good amount of solids, the first stage formulas listed above are suitable until the age of one, when he can change to cow's milk. From one year, milk makes a far less important contribution, as solids become the main part of the diet. Over the age of one, a child should be drinking a minimum of 350ml (12oz) of milk a day and not more than 500ml (17oz). They should also be eating regular meals and snacks. Drinking excessive amounts of cow's milk may lead to a poor appetite for food and possibly iron deficiency anaemia, which can cause serious problems (see page 164).

Recent scientific developments with formula milk have included adding a special type of fat – long chain polyunsaturated fatty acids (LCPs) – found in breast milk to aid brain and visual development. Some companies add nucleotides, often described as the 'building blocks' of life, to their formulas because they occur naturally in breast milk. Others include ingredients such as beta-carotene, which acts as an antioxidant (see page 110). There are also milks designed for babies with medical conditions. Those suffering with reflux, for example, can be given milks designed to thicken in the stomach to prevent them being brought up (see page 189), while babies who develop lactose intolerance after a bout of gastroenteritis may benefit from formulas that are very low in lactose.

Allergies are becoming more common, and there are now specialised milks for babies from allergic families. For example, milks to combat cow's milk protein allergy contain hydrolysed proteins, which have been chemically altered so that the body does not recognise them as foreign substances. In the past allergic babies were given soya formulas instead of cow's milk ones, but it was found that they often went on to develop an allergy to soya. For this reason, and because they contain a form of oestrogen, soya formulas are no longer recommended for most babies (see pages 157 and 162).

If you are uncertain about which milk to use, or are concerned that your baby may be drinking too much milk, consult your health visitor or other health professional.

Preparing infant formulas

Accurate preparation is essential in order to provide safe feeds for your baby. Make them too strong and you risk overloading your baby's kidneys. Make them too weak and you risk underfeeding your baby. All powdered formulas come with their own scoop for preparation purposes. As the size of these scoops can vary, always use the scoop provided with the product. The general rule is one scoop to 30ml (1oz) of cooled, boiled water. Level the scoop with the back of a clean knife, being careful not to pack the scoop tightly.

Feeds are usually prepared in the feeding bottle by adding the required number of scoops to a measured amount of water. (Always make sure that the bottle and teat have been sterilised, and that your hands and the work surface are clean.) The bottle is then sealed, shaken well and allowed to cool down before feeding.

Feeds can be made in advance and stored in the fridge for up 24 hours. Warm the bottle before feeding, either by standing it in hot water or by using an electric bottle warmer. Beware of heating bottles in a microwave as the milk may heat unevenly, causing 'hot spots' that can scald your baby's mouth. Always check the temperature of the milk before feeding it to your baby by shaking a few drops onto the inside of your wrist. Any leftover milk should be discarded.

Many manufacturers now sell their products already prepared in cartons. These are very convenient to use, as the milk simply can be poured straight into the bottle and warmed if necessary. Some companies also produce single-feed powder sachets to which you add a specified amount of water. These are convenient when you are away from home, can't easily carry bulky tins and where a clean preparation surface might not be available.

Whichever type of formula you choose, always follow the manufacturer's instructions to ensure safe and adequate feeds for your baby.

• Always make formula feeds using cooled, boiled water.

• Always sterilise bottles and teats.

Bottled water
Some parents assume that bottled mineral waters are healthier than tap water, but they can be dangerous for babies. These waters are not sterile, and babies under six months are susceptible to any harmful bacteria the water might contain. The sodium content can also be a problem: parents should always check the label to ensure that the water contains no more than 200mg per litre. All water used for feeds or given as a drink must be boiled, cooled and stored in a fridge.

Filtered and softened water
Many homes today have water filters installed, or people use filter jugs stored in the fridge. These filters remove particles from the

water but do not sterilise it. If not changed frequently enough, filters can even be breeding grounds for bacteria. For these reasons, filtered water must always be boiled for infants under six months. Freshly filtered water can be given to older babies and children. Softened water produced by an ion-exchange system contains high levels of sodium and must not be used to prepare infant formulas.

Weaning

During the first few months of life, breast or formula milk provides a baby with all the nourishment he needs, and is nutritionally adequate for up to six months. However, from four months or so, some babies may be ready for small amounts of solids. The process of expanding your baby's diet to include solids as well as milk is called 'weaning'. This is a crucial time in a baby's life and, if done correctly, can help to prevent problems such as fussy eating later on. In addition, as growth and development are happening so rapidly during this period, ensuring that your baby gets the right mix of nutrients will give him the best start in life.

Proper weaning will teach your baby to:

- Accept different foods, which might help to avoid fussiness later on.
- Learn how to bite and chew, which will also help with learning to talk.
- Use a spoon and learn to feed himself.
- Move from a bottle to drinking from a cup.
- Enjoy the social aspects of eating.

Babies should not have solids before four months because they can put a strain on the immature gut and kidneys. In addition, babies simply do not have adequate head control and coordination to accept and swallow solid foods. By six months (26 weeks), however, babies can no longer obtain all their nourishment from milk, and they require solids for essential nutrients such as iron. If weaning is delayed much beyond six months, babies might miss out on learning essential skills, such as chewing, which can cause problems later on.

When to wean?

As discussed at the beginning of this book, the latest Department of Health guidelines were published in 2003 and were prompted by the World Health Organisation recommendations. These advise exclusive breast-feeding, if possible, for the first six months of life, i.e. no solids or infant formula. Babies receiving breast-milk substitutes (infant formulas) should also delay weaning onto solids until six months. The previous D.H advice was to wean between four and six months of age, and mothers might wish to start solids at the earlier age if the appropriate signs are present (see page 88). Solids should not be given before four months (17 weeks), whether babies are breast-fed or bottle-fed.

Up to a quarter of 18-month-old children in the UK show signs of iron deficiency anaemia, so any advice that may increase the risk of anaemia should be of concern. Babies rely on the introduction of iron-containing foods at six months as their bodies' stores of iron become depleted by that age and breast milk does not have adequate levels of iron to sustain them. If breast-fed babies are weaned at six months, it is important to ensure that iron-containing foods are introduced immediately to prevent iron deficiency anaemia developing.

Bottle-fed babies should be watched closely for signs that they are ready for weaning, which might occur sooner than the current D.H guidelines. Although it is important to be aware of the recommendations, many parents choose to introduce solids before six months for perfectly valid reasons – personal, social and economic – so the advice can be treated with some flexibility.

Babies' iron stores tend to run low at around six months, so it is important to introduce iron-rich foods by then (see page 37). If you choose not to introduce solids until six months, you will need to progress quite quickly through the food groups (see

Signs that your child is ready for weaning

- Appears not to be satisfied after a good milk feed, and starts to demand feeds more frequently.
- Starts waking earlier and earlier for a feed.
- Puts hands and other objects into the mouth to explore their taste and texture.
- Shows interest in foods being eaten around him.
- Dribbles more frequently.
- Starts to chew things.

page 1) to include meat or vegetarian alternatives for their iron content.

By four months babies should have good head control and posture and can form a food bolus or 'ball' in the mouth. By five months infants can hold food and put it to their mouths, and by six months they can chew. By seven months infants can shut their mouths and refuse food. It is therefore very important to introduce solids when your baby is ready.

How to get started

At first, give only small amounts of solids, aiming to introduce different tastes and textures and not to provide significant amounts of nutrition. Give solids only once a day in the beginning. The best time to offer new tastes and textures is when your baby is hungry and both of you are relaxed. If your baby is very hungry, he may be irritable and you might need to offer a small amount of breast or formula milk to take the edge off his appetite before offering the food. Beware, however, of offering too much milk, filling your child up and then expecting him to take some solids.

For a detailed weaning plan with recipes and preparation tips please consult Gina Ford's *The Contented Little Baby Book of Weaning*.

Dylan, aged six months

Problem: Milk refusal

Cause: Introducing certain foods too early

Dylan was born three weeks early by emergency Caesarean. Although his mother, Myra, was very ill after the birth, she was determined exclusively to breast-feed Dylan. She breast-fed on demand for the first eight weeks of his life. It was nearly three weeks before he regained his birth weight and, when he was six weeks old, his weekly weight gain was very low, averaging no more than 110g (4oz) a week. He was very unsettled and crying for much of the time that he was not on the breast. Myra was becoming more and more depressed and exhausted by the endless feeding and trying to cope with a very fretful baby and two other children, and it was at this stage that she was advised to top up after each feed with formula milk.

By nine weeks Dylan was getting virtually all his feeds from the bottle. Myra had breast-fed her other two children for four months and was bitterly disappointed that she was not managing to do the same for Dylan. She contacted me for advice on how best to increase her milk supply so that Dylan would be getting most of his milk from the breast instead of the bottle. I suggested that she follow my plan for a low milk supply for one week (see *The New Contented Little Baby Book*).

As Myra's milk supply was so low, I advised that she would have to top up with formula after the 10.30am feed, instead of expressed milk as the plan suggests. Within one week her milk supply had increased so much that Dylan was taking the breast at all the daytime feeds, with a top-up of expressed milk after the 10.30am and 6.15pm feeds, and only one formula feed a day at 11pm. By the end of the 12th week Dylan was sleeping through to 7am from his last feed. He continued to feed well from the breast and gained 240g (8oz) in weight each week until he was four months old. At this stage his mother gradually began to introduce more formula milk, and by five months Dylan was on four full formula-feeds a day, and a small amount of solids at 11am and 5pm. He was also sleeping well from 7pm to around 6.30am every night.

Things continued to go well for a further five weeks. Myra was advised to begin weaning Dylan at about five months of age, and she introduced small amounts of first-stage weaning foods, plus some other fruits. However, one night Dylan suddenly woke up at 2am. Myra tried to settle him with a cuddle and some cool, boiled water but he could not be consoled. Myra was concerned that he might genuinely be hungry as he had only taken 150ml (5oz) at the 6pm feed, so she decided to offer him a small 120ml (4oz) feed. Dylan drank this quickly but still refused to settle back to sleep until he was given a further 120ml (4oz) of formula. He then settled back to sleep very quickly and had to be woken at 7am.

During the following week Dylan became more and more difficult over his day-time milk feeds, and a pattern soon emerged of him taking only 120–150ml (4–5oz) at each daytime feed, and only 90–120ml (3–4oz) at 6.15pm, before waking up desperately hungry between 2am and 3am. When his mother contacted me for further advice she assured me that she was still following my routines and guidelines to the letter.

The daily records she sent me showed that, until things had started to go wrong, the structure and timing of milk feeds and solids were correct. However, I noticed that she had decided to introduce certain fibrous foods earlier than I recommend. Banana, which I advise introducing at six months, was added to his breakfast cereal at five months. Dylan loved banana, and this prompted his mother to offer it to him regularly at lunchtime along with mashed avocado, another food that I believe is hard to digest.

In addition to the large amounts of banana and avocado that Dylan was being given, when meat was introduced at six months it had resulted in him cutting back too quickly on his milk intake. The quantity of foods that I believe take longer to digest had been introduced and increased too quickly. As a result, he had to wake in the night to make up for the milk he still needed and was no longer getting during the day. It was clear from the feeding charts that Dylan, who then weighed 6.6kg (15lb), had cut back too dramatically on his milk intake during the day because his solids had been increased too rapidly (especially at breakfast). Myra, desperate to increase the amount of milk he was taking, decided to mix more formula into his breakfast cereal, which resulted in him having eight teaspoonfuls of breakfast cereal plus mashed banana at breakfast.

I advised Myra to cut back the breakfast cereal to four teaspoonfuls, with one or two cubes of pear or peach purée instead of banana. Lunch generally consisted of six tablespoonfuls of a savoury casserole followed by rice and fruit, and was also contributing to Dylan's decreasing appetite for milk. I suggested that Myra replace the rice and fruit with fruit and yoghurt. At teatime Dylan was given another savoury dish, again usually made up of fish or chicken, mixed with rice and formula milk to help boost his milk intake. I advised her to replace the meat dish with some carbohydrates, such as pasta or a baked potato with vegetables.

Within a week Dylan had increased his three daytime milk feeds to 210–240ml (7–8oz) a feed. Although he continued to wake up during the night for a further 10 days, I convinced his mother that it was now being caused by habit rather than a genuine need for milk, and she followed my suggestion of settling him back to sleep with some cool, boiled water. At the end of two weeks Dylan was eating three well-balanced meals a day and drinking 690ml (23oz) of formula from the bottle and taking a further 120ml (4oz) of formula in his cereals.

I believe that the types of foods Dylan was first weaned on were the cause of his rapid decrease of milk. Being given too much banana and avocado, and mixing sweet potato with baby rice, during the early stages of weaning causes babies under six months to cut back too quickly on their daytime milk. In Dylan's case the problem was made even worse by the fact that he weighed only 6.6kg (15lb) and that he was being given meat twice a day as well as hard-to-digest foods.

It is a common mistake to introduce too much of the wrong types of food too early or at the wrong time and thus create a problem of milk underfeeding. It is the main reason for babies under six months cutting back too quickly on their daytime milk, which results in a genuine need to feed in the night.

Gina Ford's Top Tip
Always start weaning your baby after his second milk feed of the day. This will ensure that he does not cut down on his daily intake of milk too quickly.

First-stage foods: 6–7 months

At this stage your baby will learn to eat from a spoon and to accept a variety of flavours. Offer non-wheat cereals, such as baby rice, mixed with water, expressed breast milk or infant formula. Never add less water to the cereal than the manufacturer's instructions suggest. If it is still a bit too thick, you can add more fluid than suggested, but never less.

Next try smoothly puréed fruit and vegetables (the thickness of single cream). Let your baby get used to taking food from a spoon and accept that there will be some mess to deal with. Once he is used to the spoon, start introducing more flavours, beginning with savoury ones, such as vegetable purées, which tend to be less well accepted. Gradually expand the variety of foods being given to include puréed meat, puréed pulses (beans, peas and lentils), and increase the variety of fruits and cereals. If you use commercial foods, make sure they are intended for the first stage of weaning. Flavours that a baby rejects should be offered several times when he is hungry before you accept that he doesn't like that particular food. By the end of seven months your baby should be managing small amounts of solids for breakfast, lunch and dinner.

It is worth noting that some babies may not need to go through this purée stage if solids are started at six months. In other cultures babies go from breast or formula onto mashed family foods. Puréed foods are necessary only if starting solids before six months.

Paul Sacher's Top Tip

When feeding your child from a jar or tin, always pour the required amount into a bowl unless you know he will eat the lot. Feeding direct from a jar introduces germs from your baby's saliva on the spoon into the food, so don't seal and store it for future use: it will be full of bacteria.

Second-stage foods: 7–9 months

By this stage your baby should start learning to eat lumps and pieces of food. Continue introducing a wider range of tastes and textures, progressing to purées with soft lumps to encourage chewing. It is also important to introduce finger foods, which your baby can hold comfortably and bring to his mouth to suck or nibble on. Problems often occur at this stage as babies may not accept these new textures, or will gag when offered them. If this happens, do not make a fuss or panic – this will simply alarm your child even further.

Gina Ford's Top Tip

If your baby goes through a stage of refusing food from a spoon, try puréeing his casseroles or meat and vegetables together and spreading it on toast or small pieces of bread roll.

Allow him to cough and clear his throat of the food, then continue eating. Always supervise your baby when he is eating.

Research shows that if textured foods are not introduced at this stage, your baby is more likely to develop feeding problems later on. Family foods can be used as long as they are mashed or blended to contain some lumps. If commercial baby foods are used, those designed for the second stage of weaning are more appropriate. Introduce finger foods, such as thinly sliced strips of buttered toast, chopped banana and cooked carrots. By the end of this stage your baby should be eating three good meals every day.

Did you know?

Research has shown that babies who are not given lumpy foods by 10 months of age are more likely to have feeding difficulties later on.

Third-stage foods: 9–12 months

By the end of this stage you should be aiming for three meals plus 2–3 snacks per day. Food should be chopped or minced, and your baby should be encouraged to feed himself, even if it means you have a bit of mess to clean up. Offer finger foods, such as pieces of fruit, vegetables and cheese, with meals and as snacks. Aim to incorporate family foods as far as possible, and to include your baby in family meals. Problems arise when babies are given different foods from the rest of the family and therefore do not learn to eat the typical foods prepared at home. By one year of age your baby should be eating chopped food and self-feeding with a spoon at least some of the time.

Foods to avoid

- Avoid wheat or gluten, egg, fish, cow's milk, soya and citrus fruits if your baby is weaned before six months. This is a precaution against an allergic reaction in some susceptible children.

- Avoid nuts in any form until three years of age if there is any allergy in the family.

- Avoid whole or broken nuts until five years of age because of the risk of choking; peanut butter and blended nuts incorporated into foods are fine.

- Avoid honey until 12 months to avoid the risk of botulism – an extreme form of poisoning caused by the *Clostridium botulinum* bacterium.

- Avoid adding salt or sugar to baby foods.

Commercial baby foods vs. home-made

We recommend using home-made foods rather than commercial products, and incorporating family foods into your baby's diet as soon as you can. In tricky situations, such as when travelling or eating away from home, manufactured foods can be used but always make a point of looking at the list of ingredients on the label in order to ascertain clearly what is in the food.

Gina Ford's Top Tip

If your baby will eat food only from jars, try replacing a level teaspoonful of it with a similar home-made meal every 3–4 days until he is happy to eat a complete home-made meal.

Commercial baby foods

Advantages	Disadvantages
Composition strictly controlled by EU legislation	Unable to alter taste and texture. No control over composition or ingredients
Convenient and time-saving	Increased cost
Easy to serve when travelling or away from home	Can't take advantage of seasonal ingredients
Large range available (puréed, dried, savoury, sweet, organic, frozen)	Child may be reluctant to switch to family foods

Home-made baby foods

Advantages	Disadvantages
Less expensive	Time-consuming to prepare
Known ingredients	May not look as attractive
Easier for baby to get used to the taste of family foods	Shopping and cooking skills needed
Tastes and textures can be altered	

Labels on baby foods

Food labelling has come along in leaps and bounds over the past few years, especially on food intended for children under the age of one. These foods are often labelled with suitable age ranges, an indication of the texture and flavours that particular ages can tolerate. For example, those labelled as suitable for babies from four months are puréed and completely smooth, whereas those for babies from seven months contain lumps. For some children, however, making the transition from puréed to lumpy foods in one step is quite an ordeal, and they might need a middle ground, such as slightly thicker or finely mashed textures. This is where making your own baby foods can offer huge advantages.

Common weaning problems

When problems arise during the weaning period it is essential to solve them as quickly as possible to prevent them escalating and becoming even more difficult to solve later on.

Bottle or cup?

Babies who feed from a bottle past the age of one often have problems with dental caries and over-dependence on breast, formula or cow's milk, or juice, which can lead to a poor intake of solids. It can also be very difficult to get them to give up the bottle once they are older. Try to offer milk or water from a cup at six months of age. Using an open cup teaches a child to sip rather than suck, and is less likely to encourage excessive drinking than a covered cup with a drinking spout. Do not allow your baby to fall asleep with a bottle: feeding must be kept separate from sleeping.

Q Why does my nine-month-old baby refuse lumpy foods and eat only purées?

A Some babies are very stubborn and refuse the unfamiliar. A mistake easily made is to give in to your baby's demands and offer purées when he refuses second-stage foods because you are worried that he might go hungry. We have never seen a healthy baby starve himself, so it is important to be persistent and not allow your baby to control what he eats. Try to offer the new foods when he is very hungry, even if it means replacing the previous milk feed with some water and then waiting until the next mealtime and offering the new food. If your baby is very hungry and miserable, try offering a small milk feed to take the edge off his hunger, then try offering the new food once again. If he refuses, simply end the meal without a big fuss, but definitely don't offer the familiar food, such as the purée, or he will quickly learn that refusing a new food will make you give in to his demands.

Some babies do not like lumpy foods but will take finger foods quite well, so try offering meals consisting mainly of

finger foods and continue trying the new textures.
Research has shown that babies often need to be offered
new foods quite a few times before eventually eating them.
You could also try changing the texture of purées gradually
so that your baby does not notice a sudden change in the
consistency of the food.

Can babies chew without teeth?

It is incorrect to think that babies can't eat lumpy foods until they
have teeth; quite the opposite is true. Babies have very hard gums,
which they use to chew on soft foods. Also, allowing them foods
that require chewing will help their new teeth to come through.

Q My baby keeps gagging or coughing when I offer him
foods with lumps.

A It is important never to leave babies alone when they are
eating in case they choke. Make sure you are familiar with
the procedure for dealing with a choking baby. Having said
that, choking on foods is very rare, and as long as you are
present when your child eats, you should not be scared to
offer foods that contain lumps. Obviously, foods such as
nuts and grapes should be avoided.

A bad experience with a lump of food stuck in the
throat can be quite scary for a baby and may be enough to
make him refuse to swallow any foods containing lumps.
On the other hand, being overly cautious and not offering
your baby foods with lumps can lead to problems later on,
as learning to chew is a step on the way to learning to talk.
We have encountered families where the baby has coughed
and spluttered after eating a particular food, causing such
distress to the parents that they have reverted to puréed
foods and stayed there. Not offering foods of different

consistencies and failing to challenge your child's feeding abilities will stunt his development.

In many cases, gagging is behavioural and a baby's way of controlling what foods he will and won't eat. If your baby gags and you immediately offer him puréed food, he will quickly learn that gagging leads to a 'soft option'. If he gags, remain calm, do not make a big fuss, reassure him, then offer the food again. If your baby continually gags or coughs when being fed, he may have a medical problem and should be assessed by a speech and language therapist who is trained in swallowing and feeding problems. Speak to your GP about this.

Marietta, aged 14 months

Problem: Refusal of lumpy food

Cause: Overreaction to initial gagging

Marietta weighed nearly 4kg (9lb) at birth and very quickly regained her birth weight. She breast-fed well during the day, and slept through the night at four weeks after her formula-feed at 10pm. She continued to sleep and feed well, following *The New Contented Little Baby Book* routines to the letter until she was nearly 12 months old. Marietta was a very advanced baby both physically and mentally. She was crawling well, walking around the furniture; had developed good hand–eye coordination, and was able to pick up and examine many of her smaller toys. She particularly enjoyed the challenge of the different shape-sorter toys that she had, getting very cross if anyone attempted to help her fit the shapes into the right holes. It was at this stage (12 months) that her grandparents arrived from overseas for an extended visit of four weeks. Marietta was their first grandchild and they were keen to spend as much time as possible with her. This suited Marietta's parents well, as they were in the process of extending and renovating part of their large house, and having the grandparents present meant that Elizabeth, Marietta's mother, could then devote much more time during the day to the project, knowing that her child was being cared for by her grandparents.

Marietta had been happily and easily weaned onto a variety of solid food, and by the age of 12 months the fish, chicken and lamb she ate was either mashed or finely puréed. She was happy to eat most of her fruit and vegetables either sliced or diced. At mealtimes Elizabeth always allowed Marietta to eat a certain amount of the finger foods by herself, and would give her a spoon when offering mashed or puréed savoury foods. While mealtimes were very messy occasions with a fair amount of food going on the floor and in Marietta's hair, they were always a happy time. The minute Marietta started to refuse food Elizabeth would immediately remove her from the high chair, regardless of how much she had eaten.

For the first few days of the grandparents' visit Elizabeth went through her routine very carefully, particularly at mealtimes, so that they would know how things were done when the time came for them to look after Marietta themselves. Marietta's grandmother listened carefully to what Elizabeth had to say and assured her that she would follow the instructions to the letter.

Unfortunately, on the first day that they were left to look after Marietta for a few hours, disaster struck. As lunchtime began, Marietta gagged on a piece of fish and started to cough and splutter. She became quite hysterical, as did her grandparents, convinced that she was going to choke to death. After they had managed to calm her down, they were so petrified of giving her any more mashed fish pie or diced vegetables that they decided to blend it all up together to a smooth purée and feed it to her from a spoon. By this time I suspect that Marietta was probably exhausted from her ordeal and getting tired before her midday nap. Whatever the cause, she refused to take more than a few spoonfuls of food. Her grandparents, concerned that she had eaten very little lunch, decided to give her a bottle of formula before settling her for her nap. She took nearly 270ml (9oz) and slept soundly until 2.45pm, when she woke and took a further 240ml (8oz) of milk.

At teatime, reluctant to risk a repeat of lunchtime, Marietta's grandparents puréed all her food to a very smooth consistency. From the minute she was placed in her high chair she became fussy and fretful and shook her head from side to side when her grandparents attempted to feed her. Elizabeth arrived back midway through the meal to the sounds of a crying Marietta, Grandpa clapping and singing in Italian and Grandma holding Marietta's hands down on the high chair while trying to force her to take a spoonful of food. Hasty words were exchanged as Elizabeth lifted a screaming Marietta from the high chair. Elizabeth tried to explain to her in-laws that self-feeding is not only important for encouraging children to eat well but also plays an important part in helping them develop physical and mental skills, by encouraging hand–eye coordination, and improving their fine finger control, often referred to as the 'pincer grip'. Elizabeth had encouraged Marietta to learn all these things during her playtime, so when she was suddenly restricted from using these skills at mealtimes, it must have caused her much confusion and frustration. Elizabeth also tried to explain that at this age babies become very aware of colour and texture, and that it was important that Marietta could define the different colours and textures of her food and that she would become very bored if they went back to giving her all her food puréed in one bowl.

Grandma told Elizabeth that she had managed perfectly well to raise three happy, healthy children. By the time husband Marco arrived home that evening, his parents were packed and ready to leave. After much persuasion by Marco, his parents agreed to stay on for the duration of their planned visit. He also convinced Elizabeth to give his parents a little leeway with Marietta, as she was their only grandchild and living so far away would mean that they were not going to see her very often. He also convinced her that Marietta was such a good baby that they could easily and quickly correct any problems once his parents were gone. Marco's pleas, plus her own exhaustion from dealing with builders and work that was way behind schedule on the house renovation, persuaded Elizabeth to allow the grandparents to deal with Marietta's mealtimes as they thought best.

During the next three weeks all of Marietta's food was puréed to the smoothest consistency, and given to her by spoon. Mealtimes became more and more erratic: sometimes Marietta would eat small amounts, provided she was entertained and sung to; other times she would scream the minute the spoon went near her mouth. Her milk intake during the day increased rapidly as her solids decreased, and she became more and more addicted to fromage frais and custard puddings, which were always Grandma's answer on the days she was more difficult to feed.

By the time Marietta's grandparents left after their four-week visit, not only had Marietta gone from being a baby who would eat anything to being fussy and fretful at mealtimes and refusing all lumps, but she was also refusing to drink any milk from her cup and had reverted to having four or five milk feeds from a bottle. In addition, Marietta was no longer happy to sit and play with her toys – she expected to be entertained most of her waking hours. The relationship between Elizabeth and her husband hit an all-time low, as he had taken the view of his parents that Elizabeth had forced Marietta to do things before she was physically capable and that was the cause of the present problems. He would not accept that his parents were in any way to blame for Marietta's change from a happy, advanced, bright little baby who enjoyed a challenge to a very demanding and fussy one.

Elizabeth contacted me at this point. I assured her that Marietta's behaviour had been caused by her grandparents' overreaction. I explained that very young children can sometimes become quite upset by the surprise of finding a lump in their food. It can make them uncertain about what to expect in a mouthful, so they sometimes refuse foods that aren't smooth. For this reason, I advised her to continue giving Marietta the majority of her food puréed, but gradually to introduce small finger foods that she could feed herself and that wouldn't take her by surprise. After a while, Elizabeth introduced some diced vegetables with the purée, and gradually built up the amount of lumpiness until Marietta's meal consisted entirely of chopped and diced food.

Once Marietta was happily eating a wide variety of different foods in this way, we started to reintroduce proteins in a lumpier form, beginning with fish. Marietta's parents were delighted with her progress, and her father recognised that he should have been more supportive of his wife's wish to eliminate less nutritious food from Marietta's diet.

Within a further 2–3 weeks, Marietta was happily taking flakes of fish, and then quickly progressed to shepherd's pie and meatballs in tomato sauce. Although it took several more weeks, she was happily eating a variety of meals, including home-made chicken nuggets, chopped chicken and lamb, by the time she was 18 months.

Many children will happily progress from puréed food to mashed to pulsed and then to eating normally. Yet there are those children who will gag on food with lumps, particularly protein food. If you find your child is susceptible to gagging, it is important not to force him to eat food of this consistency since this can exacerbate the problem. Continue to purée protein food carefully, but feed the child this together with other vegetables they can feed themselves. This enables them to eat solid food without gagging.

Feeding Older Babies and Children

It can be difficult moving from one feeding stage to the next, and questions arise as to the correct quantities of food growing children need. The table opposite is intended only as a guide. Remember that some children will eat little one day and then much more the next.

Dangerous foods for toddlers

Toddlers will pick up and taste almost anything that comes to hand, including insects, soap and sand. They will generally learn very quickly which foods taste good and which don't. There are, however, many household products that can cause nasty injuries, so never leave anything like this at eye level or in a place that little hands can reach. Always put them away immediately after use.

Take care when offering the following foods to young children:

- Popcorn is the number one food that causes choking because it is light and fluffy and easily breathed into the lungs instead of being swallowed.

- Olives are a hazard, unless stoned, and even then the odd stone can be overlooked, so it's best to avoid them.

- Hard foods, such as pieces of cheese and apple, can become lodged in the throat.

- Whole nuts, grapes and cherry tomatoes can cause choking.

- Very hot food can burn mouths and throats, so allow them to cool before serving. Children never think before touching or eating.

Make sure you learn how to deal with a choking baby by asking your GP or health visitor.

Daily portion recommendations for children

	1 year	2–3 years	3–6 years
Meal pattern	3 small meals and 2 snacks plus milk	3 meals and 2–3 snacks or milky drinks	3 meals and 1–2 snacks or milky drinks
Meat, fish, chicken, etc.	½–1 tablespoon minced or finely chopped, with gravy or sauce; ½–1 hard-cooked egg	1½ tablespoons chopped; 1 fish finger; 1 sausage; egg	2–3 tablespoons; 1–2 fish fingers or sausages
Cheese	15g (½oz) grated	25–30g (¾–1oz) cubed or grated	30–45g (1–1½oz)
Potato	1 tablespoon mashed	1–2 tablespoons; 6 smallish chips	2–3 tablespoons; 8–10 chips
Vegetables	1 tablespoon soft or mashed	1–2 tablespoons; or small chopped salad	2–3 tablespoons
Fruit	½–1 piece (45–90g/1½–3oz)	1 piece (90–100g/3–3½oz)	1 piece (100g/3½oz)
Dessert (custard, yoghurt)	2 tablespoons	2–3 tablespoons	4 tablespoons; 1 carton yoghurt (150g/5oz)
Bread	½–1 thin slice	1 large slice	1–2 large slices
Breakfast cereal	1 tablespoon; ½ Weetabix	1–1½ tablespoons; 1 Weetabix	2–3 tablespoons; 1½ Weetabix
Drinks	¾ teacup (100ml/3½oz)	1 teacup (150ml/5oz)	1 teacup (150ml/5oz)
Milk	500ml (17oz) full-fat per day (minimum 350ml/12oz per day)	350ml (12oz) full-fat or semi-skimmed per day	350ml (12oz) full-fat, semi-skimmed or skimmed per day (over 5 years)

Source: *Clinical Paediatric Dietetics* by V. Shaw and M. Lawson (eds), 2nd edition, Blackwell Science, 2001.

Peanuts

It is best to avoid giving peanuts to children under five years of age because their shape presents a risk of choking. Peanuts are just about the right size to stick in a child's throat and block the airway. It is also advisable to avoid giving them to children in families that have a history of peanut allergy.

Similarly, do not introduce peanut butter until three years of age if your child or family has a history of allergy.

- Peanut butter is a very nutritious snack food, high in fat, so a good source of energy for growing children.
- The type of fat found in peanuts is less artery-clogging than animal fats.
- If your child is gaining excessive weight, it might be wise to reduce the amount of peanut butter in the diet because it is high in fat.

Food labelling

When you shop for foods, what makes you decide which ones to put in your trolley? Some people are attracted to seductive packaging that makes the content look delicious; others are beguiled by the manufacturers' claims, often designed to sell rather than inform; children, meanwhile, are drawn to those that have catchy names or pictures of cute cartoon characters.

There are rows and rows of foods to choose from – in fact, up to 30,000 different products are on sale nowadays in the average supermarket. Compare this to the 5,000 available in the 1950s. With this abundance of choice, how can you pick the healthiest and most nutritious options? The answer lies in interpreting what it says on the packaging – the only way to determine the real value of what's inside. Did you know, for example, that 'fruit drink' is only a poor relation of 'fruit juice'? Often containing just a small amount of concentrated or frozen fruit juice (lower in vitamins than fresh), it's bulked up with water and sugar – hardly a healthy option.

Fortunately, there are strict guidelines as to what manufacturers can actually claim about their products. Follow the simple rules outlined below and it can be quite easy to see through the marketing jumble and get the healthiest foods for the best value.

Q What information appears on labels?

A The EU has very good safety rules about food
information. Every packaged food product must clearly
state the name of the food, and often the country of origin
is also named. False statements are not allowed, so claims
such as 'low in fat' must be backed up by the information
on the nutrition panel (see below). Storage instructions,
such as 'keep refrigerated' or 'do not freeze', must appear,
as must instructions for use. Other obligatory information
includes the 'sell by' or 'best by' date, the weight of the
product and the name and address of the manufacturer,
packer or seller.

Turkey Casserole

Ingredients: turkey, potato, carrots, swede, wheat starch, corn oil, yeast extract, herbs, ascorbic acid.

Nutritional Information

TYPICAL VALUES	PER 100G
Energy	291kJ
	70kcal
Protein	2.9g
Carbohydrate	9.3g
of which sugars	1.0g
Fat	2.3g
Fibre	0.1g
Sodium	0.1g

How to store

Store in cool dry place.

Produced in the UK

Best before:

OCT 2004
L3296E
11:18

150g e

Ingredients

The list of ingredients must name everything present in the product in order of quantity, from highest to lowest. All additives, colourings and preservatives must also be listed.

Nutrition information

In the UK nutrition labelling is voluntary unless a nutrition claim, such as 'low fat' or 'high in fibre', is made. However, most packaged products provide the nutritional content of the food because consumers find it so useful. This is usually broken down into energy, protein, carbohydrate and fat, but sodium, fibre and other nutrients, such as calcium (depending on the type of food) may also appear. The figures given are per 100g or 100ml, which allows you to make direct comparisons between products. Sometimes figures per average serving are included, but remember that the average serving is for an adult, not a child.

Energy

Food is the body's fuel, which it converts into energy. This is measured in calories (kcal) or kilojoules (kJ). High-energy foods are essential for growing bodies, but the source of the energy is equally important. For example, white sugar is a good source of energy but provides nothing else and is known as an 'empty calorie' food. On the other hand canned fruit in natural juice provides energy but is loaded with vitamins, minerals and fibre. Be aware of the energy content of foods, but also note where the energy comes from (see Ingredients, previous page).

Protein

Protein is important for growing bodies, building muscles and repairing damage (see page 24). You can expect a food made from meat or pulses, or containing dairy, to be high in protein, whereas a product made mostly of wheat, such as bread, would be relatively low in it.

Carbohydrate

Although foods such as wheat, rice and potatoes most commonly spring to mind when we think of carbohydrate, sugar also belongs to this group, and it is interesting to see what proportion of the carbohydrate figure it constitutes. For example, if carbohydrate is listed as 17g and sugar as 14g, you know that 14g of the 17g is pure sugar and 3g is starch. This means that the majority of the carbohydrate comes from added sugar. In some cases, however, a high sugar content might come from the naturally sweet fruit or milk content of food rather than added sugar, so read the ingredients. (See page 26 for further information about carbohydrate.)

Fat

Fat is important for growing children as it is a good source of energy (see page 30). Generally fat from non-animal sources is the healthiest option, but fat from fish is an exception to this rule. (see page 31).

Fibre

Essential for a healthy digestive system, fibre or roughage is found in highest quantities in fresh rather than refined foods (see page 29).

Sodium

On nutrition labels salt is listed as sodium, but these two things are not the same. The sodium figure in grams must be multiplied by 2.5 to get the true salt figure. Not surprisingly, there is growing pressure from consumers and health professionals for manufacturers to change this practice and clearly state the amount of salt. (See page 39 for recommendations on the maximum amounts your child should have.)

Did you know?
The Food Standards Agency gives the following advice on the sugar, fat and salt content per 100g of children's food:

A little	A lot
2g of sugar or less	10g of sugar or more
3g of fat or less	20g of fat or more
0.1g of sodium (equivalent to 0.25g of salt) or less	0.5g of sodium (equivalent to 1.25g of salt) or more

Food additives

The ingredients list on food packaging must include by name or E number any food additives present. Although additives are checked for safety and their use is tightly regulated, it is known that some people cannot tolerate them. Certain additives have been associated with hyperactivity and behavioural problems in children, but it is very difficult to establish how common this is and which are the offending substances (see page 160). Food additives fall into the following groups.

Antioxidants

As their name suggests, antioxidants help to stop oxidation, a process that breaks down ingredients in food, especially fats. They also help the body to mop up free radicals (molecules that cause damage to our body cells), which are produced by radiation from the sun, pollution and various other harmful processes in the body. Antioxidants occur naturally in numerous foods, particularly fruit and vegetables, and are added to many manufactured foods, especially those containing fats or oils. Antioxidants help to delay the fats going rancid and changing colour. They are also used in other products, such as baked goods, sauces and soup mixes. The most common antioxidant added to food is vitamin C (also known as ascorbic acid).

Colours

Foods are often coloured to make them look more attractive. Some food colourings, such as curcumin (E100) – a yellow extract from turmeric roots, are natural, while others, such as tartrazine (E102), are artificial. The latter has been associated with adverse reactions in some children, but most artificial colourings are not thought to be a problem for the majority of children.

Emulsifiers, stabilisers, gelling agents and thickeners

A variety of ingredients are used to improve the appearance and texture of food. Emulsifiers help to combine things, such as oil and water, that would otherwise separate; stabilisers keep them together. Gelling agents help to produce a desired consistency. The most common gelling agent is pectin (E440), widely used in jam-making. Thickeners do the same job as flour in sauces – they give body to foods.

Flavour enhancers

Flavour enhancers improve the taste of foods without adding any flavour of their own. Best known of these is monosodium glutamate, otherwise known as MSG (E621), which is used in processed foods, including sauces, soups and sausages. Beware of foods containing MSG, as they may be high in sodium or salt. It is probably wise to avoid too many processed foods containing lots of artificial flavourings. Natural flavourings do not need to be detailed on lists of ingredients.

Preservatives

Extending the shelf-life of food is a constant concern among manufacturers, and preservatives are used to keep food safe to eat for longer. Sulphur dioxide (E220) is a widely used preservative, often used to protect dried fruit from bacteria.

Sweeteners

As food manufacturers attempt to reduce the sugar content in food, more and more artificial sweeteners are being used. These are tested thoroughly for safety in animals and adults, but their effects on children are uncertain, so it is probably wise to keep food and drinks containing artificial sweeteners to a minimum. Examples include cyclamate (E952), aspartame (E951) and saccharin (E954). (See page 62 Artificially sweetened drinks.)

Most additives are harmless to children in small quantities, but high amounts may cause problems in some so it is best to avoid them whenever possible. For a full list of additives and their E numbers permissible in the EU, please refer to the Food Standards Agency website: http://www.foodstandards.gov.uk/safereating/additives-branch.

Don't be fooled by marketing hype

Food marketing is a multimillion-pound industry based on making products seem desirable to the consumer. Huge amounts of time and money are spent in devising new strategies, designs and slogans to entice people into purchasing. Food labels promise 'fresh' ingredients – as if rotten ones might otherwise be used – and describe products with empty words, such as 'natural' and 'invigorating'. Peanut butter (see page 106), for example, is a 'natural' product, yet certain brands are packed with unnecessary sugar and oil. Always read ingredients lists and don't be fooled by advertising hype.

Food for the whole family

Foods cooked for the family should be introduced to your baby as early as possible in the weaning process, but don't add salt during cooking, and avoid serving processed foods that contain added salt.

Some family items, however, are not suitable for children because of their fat content. For example, semi-skimmed (low-fat) milk and skimmed (fat-free) milk should not be given to children under the ages of two and five respectively because fat is essential during the early years, when growth is most rapid (see page 30). For similar reasons, do not give under-fives any food that is labelled 'reduced fat', 'low fat' or 'fat free'. In rare circumstances, if your child is gaining excessive weight for his age or height, it may be necessary to reduce the fat in his diet slightly, but this should be done by reducing added fat, such as butter and margarine (see page 181). Note that reduced-fat products, such as fruit yoghurts, often have increased amounts of sugar to 'improve' the flavour. As an alternative, buy full-fat unflavoured yoghurt and add jam, honey or pieces of chopped-up fruit to make a tasty mixture.

The descriptions 'lite' and 'extra lite' can mean a number of things – reduced calories, fat, sugar or salt, or perhaps a lighter colour or texture. Read the ingredients and nutritional information carefully. Crisps described as 'lite', for example, have less fat than normal crisps, but are still quite fatty and tend to be more expensive. From both the nutritional and economic points of view, both varieties should not be given frequently.

Beware of foods that contain lots of added sugar. Read the nutritional information to determine exactly how much is present and look at the ingredients to see its source. Sugar goes under many different names, including sucrose, fructose, glucose and dextrose, and has many forms, including corn syrup, honey, fruit juice concentrate and molasses.

Liam, aged two years and 10 months

Problem: Sibling rivalry, erratic behaviour and excessive night-time waking

Cause: Using commercially made meals

Serena contacted me a couple of months after the birth of her twin girls. Both babies were doing well on the *Contented Little Baby* routines, sleeping until 4am from their last feed at 10.30pm. However, since the birth of the twins, their older brother, Liam, had started to wake up two or three times a night, often staying awake for an hour or so at a time. Serena was at breaking point, trying to survive on two or three hours of broken sleep a night and to cope with two babies and a very irritable Liam during the day. Since the birth of the babies, he had gone from being an extremely placid, loving little boy to one who would get angry and aggressive, frequently having outbursts of uncontrolled behaviour.

Her health visitor reassured Serena that Liam was probably feeling very insecure and jealous, suddenly finding that he had to share Mummy with not just one baby but two. She arranged for Serena to get some help with the twins twice a week from a government programme in her area called Sure Start so that she could give Liam some undivided attention. Things did improve slightly, but Liam still continued to wake up in the night and would settle back to sleep only when given a drink of fruit juice. He also continued to have uncontrollable outbursts once or twice a day. During one of these outbursts Liam scratched one baby's face so badly that she had to be taken to hospital to have the wound treated. It was at this point that Serena called me to see if I could offer any advice on how to deal with Liam's jealousy and rages.

Regardless of the type of problem a parent is experiencing and wants my help with, I always ask them to send me a feeding and sleeping diary. In my experience, a huge number of the varied problems that parents contact me about tend to be linked in some way to diet. Serena assured me that Liam had always eaten well and was given a wide variety of different foods. The only change in his diet was that she was unable to cook him as many fresh meals as she used to, and, more often than not, he would be given what she and her husband were having for lunch or dinner. In between meals he was only ever given fresh fruit and well-diluted juice.

At first glance it appeared that Liam was eating healthy food – plenty of bread, pasta and rice, along with a wide variety of different vegetables. Every day he would have chicken, fish or lamb at his main meal, and in the evening he would be given either a pasta dish or thick soup with sandwiches.

Serena assured me that this was the pattern of eating he had followed since reaching his first birthday. The only difference was that, following the birth of the twins, she did not have time to prepare as much of the food herself, but she always ensured that she did buy the best-quality commercially prepared food. She also admitted that she was allowing Liam to drink fruit squash, something that he had never had in the past.

I asked her to send me a list of the commercially pre-pared meals and foods that she was using. I purchased everything that Serena mentioned on her list and spent a morning analysing the labels and the ingredients. Although experts are divided about the effect commercially prepared food can have on young children, I am convinced that excessive amounts of such foods can adversely affect their behaviour.

Overleaf is a brief summary of the ingredients that I found listed in some of the meals that Liam was being given. I have also listed the basic ingredients that would go into a similar home-made version of the recipe. As you will see, all the commercial varieties have extra starch fillers and sugars in them. While an occasional meal containing these things would not affect the behaviour of the major-ity of children, I believe that, given on a daily basis, they possibly could. This would apply particularly to a child such as Liam, who had always been given meals that consisted of pure, fresh food without fillers, additives and suchlike. Starch fillers, maltodextrin (see page 28) and sugars are of no nutritional benefit to young children, and the main reason they are used is to boost the calorie content of the meal. This means that a child who is fed exclusively on these types of meals would probably not be receiving a properly balanced diet. A well-balanced diet consisting of a variety of foods is essential for the healthy growth of both mind and body.

Breakfast cereal: cereal grains, sugar, partially hydrogenated palm and palm kernel oil, dextrose, maize starch, glucose syrup, maltodextrin, salt, cinnamon, emulsifier, trisodium phosphate, colours (caramel, annatto), antioxidant.

Healthier option: wholegrain cereal without added sugars, starches or additives. If your child refuses these, read the labels of different cereals so that you can choose the one with the minimum of added sugar and additives.

Commercial Lancashire hotpot: water, potato 26%, lamb 14%, onion 7%, leek 7%, carrot 4%, lamb stock, flavourings, water, maltodextrin, yeast extract, vegetable extracts, beef extract, citric acid, dextrose, sunflower oil, wheat flour, modified starch, vegetable bouillon (salt, potato starch, yeast extract), milk (lactose), sugar, hydrogenated palm oil, onion powder, citric acid, dried celery, celery extract, leek extract, herbs, flavourings, spice extracts, herb extracts, pork gelatine, roasted barley malt extract, rosemary, black pepper.

Home-made Lancashire hotpot: lean fillet of lamb, chopped onion, chopped carrot, swede and potato, vegetable oil, vegetable stock, optional herbs.

Commercial shepherd's pie with baked beans: reconstituted dehydrated potato (42%, contains emulsifier – mono- and diglycerides of fatty acids), baked beans (beans, tomatoes, water, sugar, glucose syrup, salt, modified cornflour, spirit vinegar, spice extracts, herb extract), water, lamb 12%, tomato purée, onions, carrots, peas, flavourings (contain milk), modified tapioca starch, sugar, wheat flour, cream powder, colour (plain caramel), modified cornflour, salt, Worcestershire sauce, celery purée, yeast extract, spirit vinegar, herb, onion powder, spice, spice extracts, onion extract.

Home-made shepherd's pie with baked beans: lean minced beef, chicken stock, diced onion, baked beans, tomato purée, vegetable oil, potatoes, milk, butter, salt and herbs (optional).

Commercial chicken nuggets: reformed chicken, breadcrumbs (wheat flour, salt, rapeseed oil, dextrose, flour treatment agent, water), wheat flour, rusk, salt.

Home-made chicken nuggets: skinless chicken breasts, plain flour, small egg, wholemeal breadcrumbs, vegetable oil, herbs (optional), salt, chopped parsley.

Commercial fish pie: fish fillet pieces, reconstituted dried whole milk, reconstituted dried potato, water, vegetarian Cheddar cheese, double cream, butter, hydrogenated vegetable oil (contains emulsifier, lecithin and flavouring), colour (beta-carotene).

Home-made fish pie: fillets of fish, milk, butter, flour, chopped leeks, cheese, chopped egg (optional), herbs, salt.

The food diary also showed that Liam was drinking several large cups of fruit squash and eating so-called healthy cereal and milk bars each day. There are many types of fruit drink on the market, which claim to be tooth-friendly and contain no added sugar or artificial colour, and many cereal bars make claims to having similar health benefits.

Fruit drink: water, blackcurrant juice, flavourings, vitamin C, citric acid, sweeteners, stabiliser, preservative, colour.

Healthier alternative: pure fruit juice to five parts water.

Cereal bars: cereal grains, sugar, vegetable oil, sweetened condensed milk, glucose syrup, skimmed milk powder, inverted sugar syrup (sorbitol) and glycerol chocolate powder, lactose, wheat starch, reduced-fat cocoa powder, dextrose, salt, emulsifier, flavourings, vitamins.

Healthier alternative: most health shops have a selection of fruit and cereal bars without all the extra sugars and additives. Read the ingredients lists carefully.

Once Serena had a clearer understanding of what was in the types of food that Liam was eating, I explained to her how the excessive amounts of refined carbohydrate and sugar in his diet were probably affecting his blood sugar balance, causing him to have erratic mood swings and excessive night-time waking.

Processed carbohydrate, such as white flour, corn starch and wheat starch, and sugars are all very easily digested and absorbed. The ease with which food is digested and absorbed is indicated by its glycaemic index (GI). High GI foods, such as white bread and chips, are very rapidly digested and absorbed, which leads to a rapid rise in blood sugar. This causes the body to release insulin, which quickly decreases the sugar in the blood and can soon lead to hunger pangs again. Insulin is also a body-building hormone and causes excess sugar in the blood to be stored as fat, so excessive high GI foods have been implicated in the current rapid rise in obesity statistics. Low GI foods, such as apples and porridge, are digested more slowly and cause a gentle increase in blood sugar, promoting a feeling of fullness for longer.

I explained to Serena that the problem could not be solved overnight as we would gradually have to wean Liam off all the highly refined food he was having back onto a well-balanced diet of complex carbohydrates, proteins and fats. His sugary snacks and fruit drinks needed to be replaced with healthier alternatives, such as well-diluted fruit juice and fresh fruit, whole grain rice cakes with a spread, or homemade muffins or flapjacks.

The first thing I advised Serena to do was to replace all commercial snacks and drinks with healthier alternatives. Although Liam did have several tantrums about this, they were no worse than his behaviour before we started to change his diet. By the end of the first week he was having only the fruit drink when he woke in the night, and all his daytime drinks were either water or very well-diluted juice. He was also happily eating healthier snacks and joining in the cooking of home-made treats such as muffins.

During the second week Serena started to replace the commercial meals with similar home-made recipes. Again Liam made a fuss at some mealtimes, and on two occasions would not eat lunch. Serena was strong and did not give in to his demands, and by the end of the week he was having home-made meals at both lunch and tea. We then started to introduce healthier cereal options at breakfast, which proved difficult because Liam refused them. Serena did offer him alternatives of toast and spread, or fruit and yoghurt, but for five days Liam refused breakfast. Serena found this very difficult, as she was sure that not having breakfast was nutritionally damaging. I reassured her that she must not feel guilty as she was not starving Liam or refusing him food – she was giving him a choice of healthy options, and by giving in to his demands she could end up with him backtracking to a diet of unhealthy food, which in the long term would do him much more damage. It was a real battle of wills, but by the end of the week Liam was happy to eat one of the healthy breakfast cereals that he was offered.

He was now eating a very healthy diet, but was still prone to emotional outbursts, and although his number of wakings in the night had reduced to only one a week, Serena was disappointed that she was still having problems. I explained to her that while Liam's diet was the main cause of his bad behaviour and night-time waking, these problems were also caused by habit, and it could take a while longer for things to improve totally.

I suggested that she introduce a star chart to encourage Liam to sleep through the night without having the fruit drink, and for occasions when he behaved particularly well, or performed tasks without a fuss. Although it took a further three weeks to crack the nights, Liam did start to sleep right through the night and his behaviour saw a rapid improvement, with only the occasional temper tantrum (which is normal). He continues to be a very happy little boy who eats a really healthy diet. Serena and I went on to compile a healthy menu plan so that she could do a batch cook once a fortnight and combine healthy frozen meals with quick, fresh alternatives, such as risotto, pasta and stir-fries.

Developmental Stages for Eating and Drinking

Babies start sucking and swallowing before birth, while they are still in the womb: amniotic fluid is taken into the mouth and passes through the digestive tract. Learning to eat and drink is an important part of normal development for children, and does not happen in isolation. Below you will find suggested ages for the development of certain feeding behaviours, but these are simply a rough guide. Children are individuals, so they will start walking, talking and feeding at different ages, whenever they are ready.

From birth

In the early days babies feed by sucking, a process that leads onto the swallowing reflex. Without the combination of these two actions, babies would be unable to sustain themselves nutritionally. The ability to suck is crucial for latching onto the breast or teat. Babies suck at different strengths and speeds, depending on their hunger or even how awake they are.

Dribbling is very common and should not be a cause of concern. Young babies also gag or retch easily, a protective measure to ensure they don't choke. This protective measure stays with us for life and protects us from swallowing water into our lungs. Another important reflex is the cough, which helps to clear any food or liquid that enters the larynx or windpipe. This also stays with us forever and can be life-saving.

Solids

At around six months it is recommended to start weaning babies on to solids (see page 86, advice on weaning from milk). Taking solids into the mouth and swallowing requires a very different action from sucking. When foods are first introduced you should notice that your baby tends to spit the food out instead of swallowing because he is using the same action as sucking. Serving puréed food, which is tipped into the mouth using a shallow plastic spoon, allows the baby to suck in the food and then to swallow. As your baby becomes accustomed to solids, he will slowly learn to swallow in a more coordinated way. This is a very important period in feeding development, and often a messy one, too. Don't worry about the mess – it will lessen as the baby learns to eat more proficiently.

As babies become stronger, learn to hold their heads in an upright position and sit up with a bit of support, they move on to the next stage of feeding, which is chewing. At approximately six months teeth start to appear, and babies should gradually be offered thicker, lumpier food. The chewing and swallowing of lumps is linked to speech development. Babies who are kept on puréed foods may be delayed in learning to talk. Hard foods can be introduced as finger foods, but stick to those that melt in the mouth, such as toast, biscuits or soft cheese. Be careful not to leave babies alone when they are feeding in case of choking.

As babies get older and are gradually introduced to foods of a more solid texture, they learn to chew and swallow properly. Do not rush children by forcing them onto textures they are not ready for, but at the same time do not be too cautious.

Gina Ford's Top Tip

When your toddler starts to feed himself, serve him food from a bowl rather than a plate, as this will make it easier for him to get the food onto the spoon.

Development in the first year

Development	0–6 weeks	6 week–3 months	3–6 months	6–12 months	After 12 months
General body position	Lies on back with legs pulled up and head to one side	Strong enough to lift up head for short periods	Can hold head up	Can lift body up and crawl	Crawls really fast
Sitting	Unable to sit	Can't sit alone, back very rounded	Stronger but still unable to sit by himself	Can sit alone but needs to lean on hands	Sits alone
Head position	Head wobbles and needs to be supported	Head a lot steadier	When lifted up, head remains steady	Can lift head up	Good head control
Standing	Legs pull upwards when they touch the ground	Can't stand	Can't stand	Can walk if hands held	Can stand and walk unaided
Social Interaction	Sleeps a lot	Starts to laugh and follow objects with eyes	Notices noises and can pick things up	Starts to feed himself and imitates noises	Starts to say simple words, such as 'mama' and 'dada'

Bonding and feeding

From birth it is essential to make feeding a positive experience. Mealtimes are important parts of a baby's day, and provide opportunities for parents and babies to bond. Whether breast-feeding or bottle-feeding, bonding is helped if you remember the following tips:

• When feeding, hold the baby so that his face and yours are about 30cm (12in) apart. This is the distance at which new-borns can see best.

- Focus on your baby when feeding and do not be distracted by a book, television or other people in the room.

- As your baby gets older, allow some distractions, as he will constantly be searching for stimulation to satisfy his curiosity.

- Never restrain him or cover his head when feeding.

- Older children should never be force-fed. Mealtimes should always be a loving, pleasant experience for the whole family.

Teething

Although some babies are born with one or more teeth already visible, on average babies start to cut their first teeth around six months, and the process continues until about three years of age, when all the teeth have erupted. The first teeth to appear are commonly the incisors, starting with the bottom two front teeth and followed by the top two front teeth. Unfortunately, teething is often accompanied by symptoms that can distress both babies and parents. These symptoms can vary in severity and may affect your baby's appetite and intake of milk and solids.

Symptoms associated with teething

- More irritable than usual and cries more frequently.
- Rubs the cheek, indicating discomfort in the mouth area.
- Mouth ulcers.
- Drooling is heavier than usual.
- Rash on the chin due to excessive drool.
- Coughs from drool in the back of the throat.
- Constant attempts to chew on anything and everything.
- Gums look red and baby rubs them.
- Sleep is disrupted, with frequent waking and crying.
- Poor appetite and perhaps refusal to eat.
- Cheeks may appear flushed.

Note that symptoms vary from child to child. Some may experience many of the symptoms listed above, while others will not experience any.

Q How can I help to alleviate my baby's teething symptoms?

A When your baby is suffering, rubbing his gums with a clean finger or an ice cube can provide some relief. Giving him objects to bite can also help to reduce the pain, so offer teething rings (which can be cooled), sugar-free teething biscuits or rusks, breadsticks or oven-hardened bread. Other suitable foods include peeled cucumber, frozen bagels and frozen fruit, as biting on cold objects can help to numb the pain. Offer cold drinks and cold foods at feeding times.

Beware of brittle teething items that might break and cause choking. Also, avoid those made from PVC, as research seems to indicate that they could be potentially poisonous to children.

If your child is very difficult to settle and has a fever, you can give him a proprietary brand of painkilling syrup (speak to your pharmacist). There are also various anaesthetic preparations, many of them gels, which can be rubbed on the gums to numb the pain. Some also have antiseptic properties to help prevent infection around the area of the new tooth.

Remember that children should never be given aspirin.

When to see the doctor
During teething some children may develop a slight temperature that comes and goes, possibly because they are uncomfortable and distressed. A high temperature or fever is not usually a symptom of teething, so if this occurs, seek advice from your GP. If your child is inconsolable and not helped by any of the treatments mentioned above, there might be another reason for his distress, so once again seek medical advice.

Did you know?
According to current medical opinion, diarrhoea associated with teething is a myth. In general, it is very unlikely that a baby will have diarrhoea, a high fever or serious sleep problems due to teething.

Q Now that my baby has teeth, how do I look after them properly?

A Many parents do not realise how important it is to look after their baby's teeth. A healthy set of first teeth is important for your child's general health and well-being, and also for developing strong teeth in the future. We all know how painful a sore tooth can be, and visits to the dentist are never exactly pleasant, so prevention is better than cure.

Looking after your baby's teeth is really simple and will establish good habits from an early age, which will benefit your child throughout his life. Having painful or missing teeth can lead to poor nutrition because only soft foods are eaten; in severe cases food may be avoided altogether. Chewing is very important for developing strong jaw muscles that lead to straight teeth.

Tooth decay can begin right from the appearance of the first tooth, so tooth brushing should start as soon as it is visible. For very small mouths it might be easier to use a piece of gauze than a toothbrush. Otherwise, follow the advice in Chapter 1 (see page 29). Always use a toothpaste containing fluoride because it strengthens teeth and prevents tooth decay. Fluoride is quite safe, but for under-fives use a children's toothpaste that contains low levels of it. When using toothpaste, only a smear is needed to protect growing teeth. Encourage your child to spit the toothpaste out and not to rinse with water, as this will provide longer protection. Parents need to clean children's teeth until they are old enough to clean their own, usually between the ages of six and seven. Remember to change toothbrushes when the bristles become splayed – roughly every three months.

Inappropriate use of bottles can lead to tooth decay in babies. Bottles should be used only for milk or water, never for juice, even if diluted. However, milk naturally contains a sugar called lactose, and this too can cause tooth decay if left in contact with the teeth. In the normal course of events, saliva washes it away, but when children are sleeping, they produce less saliva, so the conditions are ripe for decay. For this reason, never allow a baby to fall asleep with a bottle in his mouth. Introduce an open cup at six months of age, and try using a dummy instead of a bottle to pacify your baby. Dummies are safe to use until the permanent teeth begin to erupt, but remember not to dip dummies in sweet things, such as jam, sugar or honey.

Brushing twice a day is effective to prevent tooth decay in most children, except those who constantly snack on sweet foods and drinks. If you do offer your child sweet things, try to do so at mealtimes when they are mixed with other, more tooth-protective substances in the diet.

Fussy Eaters

Are you tired of throwing unfinished meals into the bin, arguing over whether your child has eaten enough, or begging him at least to try the green thing on his plate? Many children nowadays are fussy eaters, and it sometimes seems that the harder you try to prepare new things they might enjoy, the more they refuse them.

Fussy eaters vary in severity. At the worst extreme, some might eat only pizza, chicken nuggets and chips – a diet that worries their parents, who fear they might not be getting everything they need to be healthy and grow well. Children are developing rapidly in the first few years, learning to take control of their behaviour and to exercise choice. The child who eats, say, only round foods or white foods is merely exerting his evolving sense of choice, but this can be very worrying, frustrating and annoying to his parents.

Many children become fussy eaters at some time in their lives, but usually outgrow it. The problem often arises between the ages of one and five years, but some children may start around 10 months. Things usually improve when children get older and start to eat outside the home and with other children. We've encountered many children who refuse to eat anything their parents prepare, but when at school or at friends' homes they eat like angels.

Preventing your child from becoming a fussy eater starts young. Children who are weaned appropriately on a varied diet are less likely to become fussy, but there are always exceptions to the rule. Even those weaned by the book can suddenly become fussy. Whatever the situation, don't use food as a reward or punishment, and never lose sight of the fact that children usually grow out of fussy eating and that it is not likely to have any long-term consequences. Far more damaging for your child is to have a constantly fretful and anxious parent.

Daniel, aged 10 months

Problem: Fussy feeding

Cause: Illness and teething discomfort

Freya had followed the routines in *The New Contented Little Baby Book* from when Daniel was two months old. He slept and fed well and by seven months was well established on three meals a day, consisting of a wide variety of carbohydrates, vegetables and fruits, and different types of protein, such as chicken, fish and lentils. He was also happy to take water from a cup at mealtimes, and a milk feed from a cup at the 2.30pm feed.

Although no teeth had come through at this stage, Daniel would happily munch away at pieces of toast, rusk and soft pieces of fruit or vegetable.

Daniel was an easygoing, happy little boy, but at eight months he caught his first cold, which dragged on for nearly four weeks. Although he was unsettled in the night as a result of excessive mucus and coughing, he would settle back to sleep fairly quickly when offered a drink of water. However, this period of illness coincided with him cutting two of his bottom teeth. His interest in food rapidly decreased during this time, as did his interest in milk feeds. In fact, he became very fussy about his feeding during the day, particularly his milk feeds.

On the health visitor's advice, Freya tried to increase the amount of dairy foods Daniel had to compensate for his lack of interest in milk. He would take small pieces of cheese but, unfortunately, he had become so fussy about taking food from a spoon that it was virtually impossible to give him things such as yoghurt, milk pudding or sauces. Concerned that his milk intake had now dropped to 240–300ml (8–10oz) a day, Freya reverted to giving him his 2.30pm feed from a bottle and reintroduced a 150ml (5oz) feed at 10pm to get his milk intake up to the recommended amount of 470–600ml (16–20oz) a day.

By the time Daniel had reached 10½ months, despite being cold-free for several weeks, his eating pattern had become even more erratic, with most mealtimes taking over an hour of coaxing to get him to eat even the smallest amount of food. He had gone from taking a 210ml (7oz) milk feed plus a whole Weetabix with mashed fruit and two or three toasted fingers at breakfast down to 90–120ml (3–4oz) of milk, a couple of teaspoonfuls of breakfast cereal and occasionally one small finger of toast. He would sometimes take a small piece of cheese or a rice cake at 10am, but again this was very hit and miss.

Lunchtime was usually the worst meal of the day, when Daniel would appear to be very hungry but would get upset when offered food from a spoon. Previously he would eat a good 6–8 tablespoonfuls of a protein dish mixed with potatoes or rice and vegetables followed by yoghurt and fruit or rice cakes and small pieces of cheese. He was now refusing all protein and eating only a tablespoonful of sliced or diced vegetables, or toast, or a rice cake spread with some cream cheese. On a good day he would also take a few slices of fruit. He would take only the smallest amount of diluted juice or water at 11am, and still refuse most of his 2.30pm milk feed, taking a maximum of 60–90ml (2–3oz). At 4pm he would sometimes eat a breadstick or piece of cheese along with a small drink of water, but again this was very erratic.

Tea was slightly easier, as Daniel would take pasta shapes without a sauce, or toast with cheese spread, and one or two tablespoonfuls of sliced vegetables or pieces of fruit. The amount was still less than half the quantity he used to take before he had been ill. He would then take 90–120ml (3–4oz) of milk at bedtime, followed by a further 150ml (5oz) at 10pm and sleep through till the morning.

When, at 10½ months, Daniel began to lose weight, Freya contacted me to see if I had any suggestions that could help improve his interest in food so that mealtimes were not a constant battle of coaxing and force-feeding that resulted in both mother and baby becoming distressed.

It is very common for babies to lose their appetite during an illness, and for it to take quite a while before normal eating habits resume. In Daniel's case, the problem was made worse by the fact that he was cutting his first teeth fairly late. Just prior to two teeth coming through, his gums were prone to bleeding and it was clear that he must have been in a certain amount of pain, hence his erratic behaviour – appearing to be very hungry but crying throughout the meal. Although he had two teeth top and bottom by the time Freya contacted me, I am sure that the pain he had been through had left him with a bad association regarding his food. This, combined with a habit of eating little and often while ill, was, I believe, the cause of him becoming very fussy about his food.

Aware of Freya's concern about his low milk intake and her wish not to have Daniel waking in the night due to hunger, I said that we could keep the 10pm milk feed for the following week. But it was important at some stage to drop this so that he would wake up in the morning hungry and eager to take a good milk feed and breakfast.

I suggested to Freya that we work at establishing two good solid meals a day, and the best way to do this was to cut out breakfast and all snacks between meals for the next three days. She was very apprehensive about my suggestions as she was worried that Daniel would be eating even less. I assured her that in my experience this would not be the case and, although he would be offered food less often, by restructuring his meals properly his intake of milk and solids would have increased at the end of each day.

On the first day Daniel took his usual 120ml (4oz) of milk when he awoke. I told Freya that he should not be offered any solids at breakfast time or his usual snack and drink of milk at 9.30am. However, when he showed signs of being hungry he could be offered his lunch, even if this meant bringing the time of it forward to between 10am and 11am. Daniel, in fact, went easily to 11am before showing signs of being hungry. He then happily ate six tablespoonfuls of chicken casserole from the spoon, followed by two tablespoonfuls of yoghurt and mashed fruit, and went on to have a dozen slices of kiwi and banana. He also drank 60ml (2oz) of water from his cup. Since his lunch had been brought forward, I advised Freya to offer him 120ml (4oz) of milk just prior to him going down for his lunchtime nap at 12.30pm.

He drank the whole 120ml (4oz) and slept until 2.30pm, and took a further 90ml (3oz) of milk when he awoke.

I advised Freya not to give him a snack in the afternoon, but to bring his tea forward should he show signs of being hungry earlier than 5pm. At 4.30pm Daniel began to get hungry and happily ate five tablespoonfuls of pasta with vegetables and butter, followed by two fingers of toast with cheese on. As his milk intake was very low that day, I had advised Freya to give him as much dairy as he would take at teatime. He finished off his tea with several small pieces of fruit and two slices of avocado, and 60ml (2oz) of water from his cup.

I suggested that Freya try to delay his bedtime feed to nearly 7pm if she could. He happily went to 6.45pm and, because he had eaten his tea early, he drank a 180ml (6oz) bottle of formula instead of his usual 120–150ml (4–5oz). At 10pm he drank only 60ml (2oz) of milk but slept through to 6.30am when he awoke in a great mood and took nearly 180ml (6oz) of milk.

Freya followed the same plan the next day and Daniel happily took a similar amount of solids and milk throughout the day. Having taken a bigger feed at breakfast his milk had increased that day. I suggested that we offer Daniel no more than 60ml (2oz) of milk at 10pm as he had slept through on that amount the previous night. He awoke around 6.15am the following morning and took nearly 210ml (7oz) very quickly and, as on the previous day, ate similar amounts of solids, which were offered at 11am and 4.30pm.

On the third evening, at bedtime, Daniel drank another 210ml (7oz) bottle of formula, which took his daily intake up to 600ml (20oz). I was confident that he would get through the night without a feed and advised Freya not to wake him at 10pm. He slept through until 6.30am and drank 210ml (7oz) of formula very quickly on waking.

I advised Freya that we could now begin to offer him a

small breakfast of fruit and yoghurt, but no more than two or three tablespoonfuls as we did not want to reduce his appetite for lunch and tea by giving him too much to eat first thing in the morning.

He ate his breakfast well and was happy to wait until 11.30am for his lunch, when he ate his usual six table-spoonfuls of savoury followed by a selection of finger foods. Now that his milk intake was up in the morning and the evening I advised Freya to give Daniel only 60ml (2oz) of milk prior to his lunchtime nap and to go back to offering him a drink of milk from a cup at 2.30pm so that that he would not drink so much that it would affect his appetite at teatime. He took 90ml (3oz) of milk from his cup at 2.30pm and waited happily for his tea until 4.45pm. He ate a really good tea of pasta, again, along with a selection of finger foods and had a small drink of water from his cup. As on the previous evening Daniel took a 210ml (7oz) for-mula feed at bedtime and slept well until 6.45am. Although the variety of foods that Daniel was eating was fairly lim-ited he was getting the quantities he needed each day from the different food groups.

I felt confident that we had more or less solved the problem and advised Freya gradually to increase Daniel's breakfast by a teaspoonful of dry breakfast cereal every couple of days until he was back to eating his normal amount of breakfast. As she did so, she could push his lunch forward to between 12 noon and 12.30pm, at which time she could then drop the milk feed before he went down for his nap, and gradually increase the 2.30pm milk feed. Apart from one little hiccup when Freya increased Daniel's breakfast cereal too much and too quickly, he con-tinued to eat really well.

Daniel is now nearly 15 months old, and although it took nearly three months to expand on the variety of foods that he would eat, particularly the protein, he has continued to eat really good amounts at all his meals. He cut back slightly on his milk intake at 14 months when he started to take all his milk from a cup, but I reassured Freya that this was perfectly normal and that, as long as he took a minimum of 500ml (17oz) of milk a day or the equivalent amount of other foods high in calcium, his daily requirement was being met.

Gina Ford's Top Tip

If your toddler is getting fussy and refusing food, try serving smaller portions on a bigger plate. Give him lots of praise when he eats it all. Gradually increase the portion by a tiny amount every three or four days until he is back to eating normally.

What to do about fussy eating

- Never force-feed your child. This will only make things worse in the long run. Force-feeding can be very distressing for all concerned and lead to worsening food aversion in children. They start associating food with negative feelings or thoughts, and the situation often goes from bad to worse. Meals must be happy times.

- Once your child is able to eat bite-sized pieces of solid food, stop preparing separate meals and introduce family foods as early as possible. Most things you prepare will be suitable for your baby, provided you don't add salt.

- Allow your child to taste things from your plate. Someone else's food will often look more tempting than the food in front of him.

- Never use food as a reward or punishment. Saying, 'If you don't eat your greens, you can't have any pudding' will immediately teach a child that greens are a punishment and pudding is a reward. Similarly, do not give sweets, crisps, biscuits or chocolates as treats.

- If your child refuses to eat a particular food, try not to lecture him or get upset. Simply remove his plate and try again another day. Chances are your child will get bored of his own behaviour, especially if it doesn't incite a response from you.

- Whenever possible, eat with your children as a family. Even if you serve yourself just a small portion or have a snack, it is important to eat together. If you can't eat at 5pm during the week, at least make sure you eat together at the weekends. And while you're about it, set a good example: if you don't eat vegetables, it is hypocritical to tell your child to do so.

- Serve a small quantity of food on a large plate so the meal looks attractive and your child does not feel daunted by a large portion.

- Have realistic expectations of how much your child can eat. Serve sensible amounts that you know he can finish, otherwise you are setting him up for failure, as he will not finish the food and not receive any praise.

- Invite other children round for meals, especially if you know that they are good eaters. Chances are your child will think twice before making a scene and refusing to eat.

- If your child eats at a friend's house, ask the parents to offer him exactly what they are eating and not to prepare something special for him. He will probably eat whatever he is served.

- Keep mealtimes short – no more than 20–30 minutes at most. Don't sit there battling over one mouthful.

- Do not introduce new foods at every meal. Concentrate on the ones that your child will eat, and build on these, possibly introducing a new food that is related to one they already eat. For example, if he eats bread but won't eat eggs, try making French toast. If he refuses fruit but likes ice cream, try serving them together and he is more than likely at least to try some of the fruit.

- Do not impose your tastes on your children. For example, if they want to dip vegetables in ketchup, allow them to do so, especially if it means they will actually eat the vegetables. Use your imagination and be creative.

- Talk to friends who have children of similar ages and decide as a group that you are all going to feed your children what the family eats and not prepare special food for them. It is all too easy for parents to fall into the trap of only serving foods they think the children will eat.

- If your child refuses to eat, simply remove his plate and offer nothing until the next mealtime.

- Don't let children fill up on snack foods when they come home from school. If they do, come mealtime they'll probably announce they don't like the food being served, whereas they are just full up from snacking all afternoon.

- If your child refuses to eat meals, don't offer snacks in between times. Children are only too willing to snack all day and not eat proper meals.

- All drinks at mealtimes should be given after your child has had most of the food, to prevent him filling up on liquids. Avoid offering sugary drinks or undiluted fruit juice, and keep an eye on drinks before mealtimes. Many children prefer to drink than eat if given the choice.

- Allow slightly older children (around four years of age) to serve themselves from dishes on the table, with the agreement that they at least try some of whatever they put on their plates.

- Try having meals in new environments, such as a picnic in the park or outside in the garden. Sometimes just changing the location of meals can break the pattern of fussy eating.

- Praise your child for eating new foods, just as you praise him for other good behaviour, such as doing his homework, tidying up, sharing toys or using the potty. Make eating just another behaviour that allows him to feel good.

- Use a system of goals and rewards for trying new foods and eating them. Help your child to design a star chart for each day of the week. If he has a good day and tries a new food, give him a star. When he has seven stars, he gets to choose a realistic reward, such as a trip to the zoo or a new toy. Toddlers should be given the reward following the meal and not at a later date, so have a lucky dip of small presents and allow them to choose one if they have eaten well. Remember not to punish your child if he doesn't eat, but to try again the next day.

- Try to relax and make mealtimes fun. This will reduce both your anxiety and your child's.

What if your child is already a fussy eater and mealtimes have become a battle ground?

So things are really bad: you are at your wit's end. You have tried everything you can think of, but your child simply refuses to eat certain foods. All your friends tell you to relax and that he will grow out of it, but you just can't when all he will eat is breadsticks and cheese.

By this stage, your child's behaviour and your responses are deeply ingrained. This problem has probably been around for quite a while now, perhaps even a few years. If your child is healthy and well apart from this problem, it is likely that you need to make some changes in your own behaviour and the way you handle this situation.

First, however, it is important to have your child medically examined to make sure there are no underlying medical reasons for his fussiness, and also to make sure that he is healthy. Explain your concerns to your GP. Ask for blood tests to check your child's iron levels, and have him weighed and measured to make sure he is growing properly. Do not be put off by the overworked GP who does not have time to do the proper checks. Second, if your child has not eaten a balanced or varied diet for a while, it may be advisable to start a vitamin and mineral supplement until his diet has improved (see page 32). Once you are reassured that he is well, it is time to start the following strategy.

Ending the battle

Stress is an appetite-killer for many people, including children. When your child sits down at the table to eat and knows from experience that a battle is about to begin, his stress levels automatically rise. The body releases hormones that reduce blood supply to the stomach and other areas, and appetite is reduced. Obviously, starting a meal in this condition is not conducive to healthy eating, so the first thing to do is call a truce. Of course, don't say this to the child – you don't want to alert him to your secret plan. Children are often too immature to understand the complexities of the situation they are in, so it is up to you to be cunning and consistent. Any inconsistencies in your behaviour will trigger doubt in your child's mind, and the situation will not improve.

It is also important that all the family members are aware of the situation and the changes you are making. There is nothing more confusing and destructive to a child than having two parents who give conflicting information: the child will soon see one parent as 'good' and the other as 'bad'. Both parents need to be on the same wavelength. If siblings are old enough to understand, explain what you are doing and why. If they are young, simply treat them in exactly the same way as the fussy eater.

Gina Ford's Top Tip

Once your child reaches three years of age, let him help draw up a menu plan, and create his own recipe book using pictures from magazines.

Step 1

Begin by restoring peace once again to your mealtimes. Try to extend this approach to other aspects of your family life if your child's behaviour is causing concerns in other areas. Start by eliminating the main behaviour that leads to arguments or stress in both the child and parent. As the most common area of concern for parents with fussy eaters is the lack of vegetables in the diet, we will use this as our example, but the following advice can be applied to any type of food.

Let's say you serve vegetables to your child every evening and he refuses to eat them. Begin the strategy by simply not serving him any vegetables. If he requests certain ones, serve only these and praise him for eating them as well as the rest of the meal. Meanwhile, continue to prepare your usual vegetables for the rest of the family, but do not serve any to the fussy eater. Expect him to feel quite elated by your behaviour and possibly also to feel that he has won the battle. Do not discuss your motives or anything relating to this issue: just do not serve the vegetables, and act as if nothing has happened. Try to let go of the stress you normally experience at mealtimes: simply feel relieved that there is nothing to argue about.

Continue this new behaviour for at least 1–2 weeks. Once the problem is removed, children will very quickly forget and should be more relaxed. With any luck, you will too, and mealtimes will be a lot more enjoyable. You will no doubt still be concerned about the fact that your child does not eat vegetables, but do not let this show.

Step 2

Now it's time to start the second part of the strategy. When shopping, look for a vegetable that you like, but know your child has never eaten or even seen before. Starting with something sweet is usually a good idea, so try a sweet potato or butternut squash. Both can be baked in the oven, whole or sliced, but have a trial run at home during the day to make sure that it is prepared properly and tastes good. Serve it at the table with the rest of the meal. Do not offer your child any and have a general conversation about the vegetable. Talk about where it comes from, where it grows – under the ground or on a tree – what the shape reminds you of, what the colour resembles, anything to make the vegetable sound intriguing. You could do an Internet search to gather some interesting information to discuss at the table. Children have vivid imaginations, and if you can trigger their curiosity, they are more likely to try something new.

Do not expect your child to try the vegetable the first time it appears, but continue to introduce new vegetables, or simply prepare the more familiar ones in different ways. Never offer your child some, or even suggest that he tries it, because this will no doubt have the opposite effect. Eventually most children will ask to taste some – and there are even children who will sneak into the kitchen after the meal to try some of the leftovers.

If your child won't eat any cooked vegetables, offer them raw, as crudités, which children often prefer. Cut them into bite-sized pieces and serve with a familiar dip, such as salsa, hummus, cream cheese or mayonnaise. Simply place them on the dining table when your child comes home from school, or on a table in a room where you know he will spend some time, and see what happens. If unsuccessful, try again when a friend comes to visit. Often the friend will tuck in, and your child, not wanting to seem 'uncool', will follow suit.

If fruit is the area of concern, try preparing a plate of cut-up fruit and simply placing it in the fridge at your child's eye-level. Chances are, when he opens the fridge looking for something to nibble, he will be tempted to pop a piece into his mouth. Remember that children, like many adults, are innately lazy when it comes to food preparation. They tend to follow the path of least resistance: it is much easier to gobble a biscuit than to eat a whole apple. Slice fruit into portions that can be held and eaten comfortably. Try serving fruit with a dip, such as flavoured yoghurt or custard, or with some ice cream.

Stay the course

When trying to end the battle, it is important for parents (and even siblings, if they are old enough) to be consistent. Bad eating habits are often years in the making and will not disappear overnight, so be patient. Children can be very stubborn, and it takes a lot of courage and willpower not to give in to their demands. Often improvements made using the methods described earlier can later spill over into other areas, such as housework or schoolwork. Be persistent and your efforts will be rewarded. However difficult it feels, don't give up – eventually things will start to improve.

Snacking

One of the easiest bad habits to develop – and one of the most difficult to break – is that of unhealthy snacking. Children between the ages of two and five are extremely active and continually on the go. They are either busy as bees or asleep. For some, sitting still long enough to eat a meal is near impossible. With such short attention spans and so much energy, finishing a plate of food is a rare occurrence. Others will sit and eat, but at this age can manage only small portions. Snacks, therefore, play an important role in bridging the gaps between meals.

However, it is very easy to get into bad habits when it comes to snacks, either with the timing or the type of foods and drinks given. Many parents struggle to find healthy snacks when not at home, particularly when surrounded by numerous fast food outlets. The temptation to pop into a newsagent or petrol station to buy a sugary drink, packet of crisps or sweets is very strong because it is usually the easiest option. Unfortunately, it is also the most inappropriate, especially if done on a regular basis.

A problem seen quite often is when a child is looked after by different carers, such as divorced or separated parents, grandparents, childminders, au pairs or babysitters. Sometimes one person gives all the 'naughty' snacks, while another goes to a lot of effort to prepare healthy, nutritious snacks, only to have the child throw them on the floor and have a temper tantrum. When food is used to bribe, reward and spoil children it creates a very tricky situation. It is very important that everyone who looks after your child is 'playing by the same rules' in order to maintain consistency and avoid confusing the child.

Giving snacks at the same time every day will help to get your child into a routine, such as having three meals and 2–3 snacks, depending on his age. If a meal is not eaten and a filling snack offered within a couple of hours of the next meal, children are unlikely to have an appetite for the meal, and this can lead to a vicious circle of refusing meals and filling up on snacks. For some families this can be fine if nutritious snacks, such as sandwiches, yoghurts and fruit, are eaten, but if meals are replaced with high-fat, sugary and/or salty snacks, your child will be losing out on essential nutrients.

Many parents feel that if their child is eating nutritious family meals, it is not important if junk foods are eaten in between. This is incorrect. Children get hungry between meals because they are growing and need nutritious snacks to build healthy bones and muscles, and to provide the vitamins and minerals needed for all the bodily processes, including brain development. Foods such as sweets, crisps and chocolate should not be a regular part of a child's diet, but things that are offered occasionally, and not used as rewards or punishment for certain behaviours. Occasional foods high in fat, sugar and salt will do no harm, but regular use will lay the foundations for health problems later in life.

Healthy snack ideas

Fruit is nature's own snack box, tasty and packed full of goodness. Most children aged 2–5 cannot manage a whole apple, but if it's cut into slices, they will often be tempted to munch away quite happily. An orange or satsuma peeled and broken into segments makes a delicious snack. Grapes are sweet and juicy and often loved by children (but beware of choking). Try offering exotic fruits when they are in season and at affordable prices in the supermarkets. The look on a child's face the first time he tries a piece of mango or pineapple is unforgettable. Let him help in choosing the fruit when you are shopping, feeling it for ripeness. Let him help to prepare it and then sit down to enjoy it. A good idea is to have a bowl of cut-up fruit in the fridge so that all members of the family are tempted to snack on it when they go in search of a tasty treat.

During the summer, frozen fruit is a simple way to encourage fruit as a snack. Simply wrap the fruit in clingfilm and place in the freezer until frozen solid. Try using grapes, orange segments, slices of pineapple, mango or watermelon, a peeled banana, or any other fruit that your child likes. Another good idea is to blend up any leftover fruit, possibly with some yoghurt or ice cream, then place it in the freezer for a tasty frozen treat, or leave it in the fridge for a delicious smoothie.

Bread, preferably wholemeal or wholegrain, can be used in many ways to make nutritious snacks. Wholemeal pitta breads are great for stuffing and, if sliced and placed under the grill for a few minutes, make delicious, crunchy snacks, great with a dip, such as hummus. Try toasting bread, spreading it lightly with butter, margarine or peanut butter and slicing it into 'fingers'. However, watch giving bread too close to main mealtimes as it can affect a child's appetite.

Some children like bland food, so try using cream cheese spread on either fresh or toasted bread. Avocado, mashed with a little lemon juice, also makes a nutritious spread. For a sweet alternative, use some jam, preferably a variety without added sugar (read the list of ingredients). Wholemeal or fruit muffins make a tasty treat.

Most children love yoghurt, but try to avoid giving them the low-fat, high-sugar varieties. Ideally, buy natural yoghurt and add your own flavourings, such as no-added-sugar jam or chopped-up pieces of fruit. This makes a wholesome snack, packed with vitamins and calcium for strong bones.

Cheese is a nutritious food and comes in many varieties, all with different flavours. Some children like mild cheeses, while others will eat even the strongest of Cheddars. Try serving thin strips of cheese on fingers of toast, or offer cubes to nibble. Cheese, like

---

Paul Sacher's Top Tip

When spreading toast or sandwiches with peanut butter, do not add any butter or margarine, as peanut butter already contains lots of fat. Your child will require extra fat only if his growth is poor.

bread, can be filling so watch how much you give to your child before key meal times.

Children often refuse cooked vegetables as they move from baby foods to more grown-up ones. Perhaps the taste of the cooked vegetables reminds them of the bland baby foods they ate in the early days. In this case, try serving raw vegetables: they're packed full of goodness and make great snack foods. Serve them with dips such as salsa, cream cheese, hummus and guacamole. Carrot sticks have great appeal because of their sweet taste. Celery sticks are less appealing, but try filling the groove with cream cheese or peanut butter for a tasty and healthy treat.

3
Special Diets for Children

Vegetarian Diet

Many families nowadays choose to follow vegetarian diets for religious, ethical or health reasons. A vegetarian diet, if followed correctly, offers many health benefits, including protection against illnesses such as heart disease and some types of cancer. Whenever foods are avoided or eliminated from the diet, it is important to make sure they are replaced with suitable alternatives. Not eating meat, for example, may cause the body's iron levels to fall, and there is a danger of developing iron deficiency anaemia (see page 164). Meat must therefore be replaced with suitable iron-containing alternatives.

Being rich in vegetables, vegetarian diets are high in fibre, which is fine for adults but not for children. Too much fibre can fill a child up prematurely and also inhibit the absorption of some minerals in the diet. To avoid too much fibre intake in children who are vegetarian, you can serve white bread and pasta in preference to wholemeal varieties.

Babies under the age of one

Infants from vegetarian families should be breast-fed, or bottle-fed a suitable infant formula (see page 5). Wean as normal and introduce vegetarian sources of protein at six months. Use dairy products, such as yoghurt and cheese, as recommended for normal weaning diets.

Instead of adding water to powdered baby foods or baby rice, add expressed breast milk or infant formula to increase milk intake.

Babies over one year

As a preventive measure against anaemia and weak bones, change to a follow-on formula instead of introducing cow's milk as a drink. Follow-on formula is higher in iron and vitamin D, both of which may be low in vegetarian diets.

Children aged 2-6

Vegetarian children require all the essential nutrients outlined in Chapter 1. Follow the guidelines below to make sure your child is getting everything he needs in his vegetarian diet.

Protein-rich vegetarian foods

Alternatives to meat

Pulses (peas, beans, lentils), nuts (see page 106, Peanuts), seeds, eggs, soya, mycoprotein (Quorn™) and wheat protein are good alternatives to meat. Include a minimum of 2–3 portions daily for your child. (See page 16 for information about portions.)

Warning: Do not give whole nuts to children under five years of age as they can cause choking.

Paul Sacher's Top Tip

Eat pulses with foods from the cereal group because eating them together provides the essential amino acids that non-vegetarians get from meat. Possible combinations include baked beans on toast and dahl (lentils) with rice.

Milk and dairy products

Milk, cheese and eggs are good sources of calcium, protein and vitamins. Include three portions daily (see pages 1–17 for information about portion sizes).

Bread, cereals and potatoes
Starchy foods are the basis of most meals, and supply carbohydrate, fibre and some vitamins and minerals. Look for breakfast cereals with added iron, such as Weetabix, Shredded Wheat and cornflakes. Use wholemeal flour and wholemeal bread, but beware of giving too many high-fibre foods to babies (see page 29). Aim for a minimum of 3–4 portions daily of starchy foods.

Fruit and vegetables
Fresh, frozen, canned, dried or juiced fruit and vegetables all supply vitamins, minerals and fibre. Potatoes do not count in this group, as they are predominantly a starchy food. Try to ensure your child gets five portions daily (see page 8 for information about portion sizes).

Iron-rich foods for vegetarians
Wholemeal bread and flour, millet flour, whole grains, fortified breakfast cereals, rice flakes, puffed rice, whole pulses, such as beans and chickpeas, and sprouted pulses are all good sources of iron.

You will also find iron in leafy greens, such as spinach, radish tops, leeks and mint leaves, and in dried fruit (apricots, dates and raisins), nuts (almonds, cashews, peanuts (see page 106) and pistachios) and seeds (sesame).

Iron is absorbed more efficiently by the body if combined with vitamin C, so offer a food or drink high in this vitamin at each meal. Tea stops the body from absorbing iron in the diet, so do not drink it with meals and do not give it to children.

Vitamin C-rich foods
You will find plenty of vitamin C in most fruit, but especially citrus fruits, such as oranges, mandarins, grapefruit, tangerines, satsumas, lemons and limes. Vegetables, such as broccoli, spring greens and carrots, are also rich in this essential vitamin. As cooking vegetables reduces their vitamin content, steam them or boil for a very short time in as little water as possible.

Vegan Diet

Vegans do not eat any animal products whatsoever. Their diet consists of fruit, vegetables, grains and pulses. Although this seems very limited, a vegan diet can be nutritionally sound if the person buying and preparing the food is sufficiently knowledgeable about combining food groups to provide complete sources of protein. Mixing pulses, such as chickpeas, with foods from the cereal family, such as couscous, will provide a good source of protein. The diet tends to be bulky as it is very high in fibre, and great care must be taken to avoid deficiencies in calcium, iron and vitamins D and B_{12}, which non-vegans get from dairy produce and meat.

Parents keen to raise their children as vegans should, if possible, make breast-feeding their first choice. When breast-feeding ceases, introduce a soya infant formula under the age of one, and continue with it for as long as possible because it is a good source of protein, vitamins, minerals and trace elements. If breast-feeding is not possible, soya infant formula is the only alternative because other non-animal milks are not nutritionally complete. If you decide not to continue with the soya infant formula after the age of one, introduce a calcium-fortified drink, such as soya, rice, oat or nut milk, but make sure you avoid the low-fat varieties.

Monitor your child's growth carefully and have regular check-ups with your GP. If you are concerned about your child's diet, seek help from a paediatric dietitian (see page 201).

Exclusion Diets

There has been much press coverage about diets that exclude such things as cow's milk, wheat, gluten and even artificial colourings and preservatives. In fact, some nutritionists recommend exclusion diets for a whole host of conditions, but may offer little follow-up and support to maintain an adequate diet. It is therefore important to seek help from an appropriate source.

State registered dietitians (SRDs) can provide advice on all aspects of eating and diet, including special diets for medical conditions. Dietitians who are state registered are regulated by the government. The professional association for dietitians is the British Dietetic Association (BDA). You can contact a state-registered dietitian through your local hospital or GP or by contacting the BDA (see page 203).

A lot of studies have looked at using exclusion diets to alleviate conditions such as hives, eczema, tummy problems and even autism, but there is still much debate about their effectiveness. It is very important to realise that these diets are medical treatments, which should be prescribed only by a doctor and explained to you by a dietitian. Do not be tempted to go it alone and exclude foods when you have no understanding of what to replace them with. Dietitians working in children's hospitals have many horror stories about children suffering from weak bones, poor growth and even malnutrition thanks to well-intentioned but ill-informed parents placing them on exclusion diets.

If you suspect that your child has a food allergy, please seek professional medical advice before making any changes to your child's food intake (see page 157).

Weight-loss Diets

Excess weight and obesity (see page 179) are affecting more and more people, and bringing a whole raft of problems in their wake, including heart disease, diabetes and cancer. Research has shown that children who become obese are more than likely to become obese adults. In addition, very overweight children tend to get teased and bullied, suffer more stress and depression, and even have higher rates of suicide than other children.

Many factors can lead to children becoming overweight or obese, including lack of exercise, spending too much time watching television or playing computer games, eating the wrong types of food, eating too much and snacking too frequently. In addition, overweight and obese children often have parents who are in a similar position.

Weight loss is not recommended for children under seven years of age. Instead, it is better to keep their weight constant as they grow taller. Diets are advised only for older obese children, and must be followed under medical supervision. These involve restricting the types and amounts of food they eat, while maintaining their intake of all the nutrients listed in Chapter 1. Without adequate intakes of such things as protein, vitamins and minerals, their height, brain and visual development can all be adversely affected. The immune system can also become weaker if children lose a lot of weight rapidly. Diets that advocate high protein and low carbohydrate are definitely not suitable for children, and can even be very dangerous. Children need lots of carbohydrates to give them energy and provide fuel for their brains.

As weight-loss diets are difficult to stay on forever, it is up to parents to encourage healthy eating and to be more active on a daily basis. This is the best way to successfully manage everyone's weight.

If you feel that you already serve the right types of food but your child is still overweight, maybe the problem lies in the size of the portions being eaten and a lack of exercise. Whatever the case, do not get obsessed with your child's weight. Apart from causing anxiety in your child, numbers on a scale do not tell you very much. It is impossible, for example, to tell what proportions are water, fat and muscle. Remember that weight gain is normal for children because they are growing.

Ways to reduce unhealthy fat in the diet for children over five

- Stick to low-fat or fat-free dairy products, but read the labels to make sure they aren't loaded with sugar to compensate for the lower levels of fat.

- Do not fry foods – bake, grill or steam them instead.

- Spread butter, margarine or mayonnaise thinly. (It doesn't matter whether you use butter or margarine as the amount used should be small.)

- Choose lean cuts of meat and remove any visible fat.

- Remove the skin from chicken before cooking.

- Read labels and avoid foods with fats near the beginning of the ingredients list. (Ingredients are listed in order of quantity in the product.)

- Replace crisps, sweets and chocolate with healthy alternatives (see page 00).

Diets Outside the Home

When it's time to go back to work and leave your child with someone else during the day, you must feel confident that you have chosen the appropriate child care. Of course, there are many factors to be considered, but do make sure you don't overlook nutrition. Some children spend up to 10 hours a day in the care of someone else, and no matter how well fed they are at home, all benefits can be lost if good nutrition is not provided. A varied and balanced diet is an important way to protect your child's health and promote growth and development. Good nutrition can also help children to improve their concentration and fulfil their potential.

Check out what your child will be fed during the day. The types of meal provided will vary, depending on the amount of time he is going to spend at the child care venue and what feeding facilities are available. Small venues, for example, might not have facilities to prepare hot meals, so they might rely on parents supplying packed lunches. Care must be taken not to confuse young children by providing them with food different from what they are used to at home. Also, giving them snacks, perhaps biscuits, that are not allowed at home could confuse them and undermine your rules. It is also important to look at the daily routine. Meals and naps at very different times can upset the patterns you've established and cause problems. In the final analysis, weigh up all the considerations and opt for the child care that most closely matches what you do at home.

Q What should I look for in nursery nutrition?

A In 2000 the Department for Education and Employment published a guide called *Healthy School Lunches*, specifying what nursery schools should provide for children in their care. It suggests that parents should look at the following points:

- What sort of food is supplied to the children?
- Ask to see a week's menu and check that it is balanced and offers plenty of variety.
- Check that the meals provide good levels of energy for growth and development, plenty of fruit and vegetables, foods rich in iron and calcium, and not too many sugary items.
- Free drinking water should be available all day.
- Drinking milk should be an option every day.

If your child has specific dietary requirements, make sure that these can be catered for, and check whether the staff are trained in the provision of special diets. If your child has a peanut allergy, it is imperative that the whole facility is nut free and that other parents are told not to send their children to nursery with peanuts in packed lunches or as snacks in case your child accidentally touches or eats one. If your child has any special medicine to treat allergies, make sure the nursery, child minder or day-care centre has a supply and that someone is trained how to give it.

Charlotte, aged 14 months

Problem: Refusal of food at lunchtime and teatime

Causes: Imbalance in types of food and snacking

Charlotte had always been a good feeder, and when weaned onto solids she would eat a wide variety of different vegetables and fruit. By seven months of age she was on three good meals a day, happily taking different types of protein at lunchtime, and took easily to different finger foods and chopped food when introduced.

When Charlotte was just over a year old her mother, Lisa, returned to work full time and Charlotte went to nursery five days a week from 8.30am until 5pm. She would have her breakfast at home followed by lunch and tea at the nursery. Within a couple of weeks of Charlotte attending nursery, Lisa noticed that she was becoming more and more fussy about her food, particularly at lunch and teatime. The nursery staff assured Lisa that this behaviour was very normal at around this age and it was a time when many children naturally cut back on the amount of food they ate, as their growth rate slowed down during the second year.

However, over the next few weeks Charlotte's feeding got so bad at lunchtime that she started to scream after a couple of spoonfuls, and she had gone from happily chewing bite-sized pieces of chicken, lamb and fish to refusing all protein whatsoever.

At the nursery teatime of 4pm, Charlotte would eat a little but rarely more than a couple of teaspoons of pasta or some other savoury dish followed by half a breadstick or rice cake and perhaps a small fromage frais. When her mother picked her up at 5pm she would then try to coax Charlotte to eat because she knew that she had had very little at the nursery. However, the more she tried to get Charlotte to eat, the worse the screaming became. Lisa came to dread picking up Charlotte from the nursery as she knew it would be followed by a battle of trying to get her to eat something before she went to bed. By the time bedtime came Charlotte was normally so exhausted from screaming and fighting that she would fall asleep after drinking only 120–150ml (4–5oz) of her bedtime milk drink.

By the time she reached 14 months, the only food that

Charlotte would eat happily was the cereal and toast that she had at breakfast. Lisa, very concerned that Charlotte had refused all forms of animal protein and was eating only tiny amounts of fruit and vegetables for over a month, rang me for advice on how to get her eating happily again.

I asked Lisa to keep a diary of everything that Charlotte ate and drank over the next three days and, very importantly, the times that everything was consumed. I explained that the timing of food and drinks was probably the cause of Charlotte's refusal to eat meat or fish rather than a sudden dislike of it. I have become convinced of this because of the high number of calls I get from parents experiencing similar problems. They report that their babies always ate well and happily, taking a wide variety of foods, until they attended nursery. I believe that one of the contributing causes of this problem is that the majority of nurseries tend to give babies and toddlers their tea at 4pm, which, in my opinion, is much too early for a child to have their last meal of the day, particularly if parents do not offer them a snack an hour or so prior to bedtime.

I was sure that this was the start of Charlotte's problem, and when I received her food diary the amount she was eating confirmed this. Although Lisa did not realise it, Charlotte was eating excessive amounts of food at breakfast. After a drink of 210ml (7oz) of milk, she would eat 2–3 tablespoonfuls of breakfast cereal mixed with milk and fruit, followed by a slice of toast with cheese spread or mashed banana, and would often go on to have a fromage frais. Without realising it, Charlotte's breakfast had steadily become bigger and bigger once her teatime had been brought forward from 5pm to 4pm when she started nursery.

This huge breakfast, along with a drink of juice and a biscuit at 10am, was, I felt, the reason that Charlotte had started to refuse her lunch. As she ate little or no lunch she was given a drink of milk and a biscuit at 2.30pm. The amount of milk, she drank had gradually increased in volume, and it wasn't until the nursery started to measure out the amount being consumed at 2.30pm that they realised it was 210–270ml (7–9oz). This huge amount of milk meant that she would eat only very little when the nursery, and then her mother, tried to feed her between 4pm and 6pm. All this meant that Charlotte was so hungry by the morning that she was taking excessive amounts of food at her first meal of the day. Breakfast filled her up so much that she was not hungry enough for lunch, and a vicious circle soon evolved of her eating and drinking too much of the wrong foods at the wrong times.

I advised Lisa to give Charlotte the same volume of food at breakfast but to make it up from fruit and yoghurt and cut out cereal for three days. Charlotte should not be given a biscuit in the morning, only a drink of juice, and her lunch should be brought forward slightly to 11/11.30am when she would show signs of hunger. Within three days Charlotte was back to eating and enjoying a well-balanced meal of chicken or fish with vegetables and a serving of carbohydrates at lunchtime. This meant that she was no longer hungry at 2.30pm and was happy to take just a drink of well-diluted juice and a piece of fruit. At 4pm she would have tea at the nursery but I advised her mother to request slightly smaller portions for her so that she would then take a second helping of carbohydrates between 5pm and 6pm.

Having something to eat slightly later in the day, not getting so overwrought at bedtime and taking a larger drink of milk at bedtime meant that Charlotte did not wake up so hungry in the morning. By the fourth day Lisa reintroduced a serving of breakfast cereal and reduced the fruit. Charlotte also had 150–180ml (5–6oz) of milk.

The problem of suddenly refusing lunch is a very common one and is rarely caused by a sudden dislike of protein but by an imbalance in the types of foods, which are often given at the wrong times. I always advise parents to ensure that they enrol their young babies or toddlers in a nursery that is willing to keep a detailed food and fluid diary and that will make minor changes, if necessary, to fit in with an individual child's needs.

4
Nutrition-related Medical Problems

It is normal for children to refuse food when they are unwell. However, if you control their temperature with suitable medication (as recommended by your GP or pharmacist), they can often be persuaded to eat and drink small amounts. If your child's illness lasts for just a couple of days, there is no need to worry; but if during that time he is vomiting and not taking fluids, contact your GP immediately.

If your child is on the small side, is unwell for longer than a couple of days and has a poor appetite, you need to try giving him small, frequent meals. Offer his favourite foods and treats, provided they are easy to chew and swallow. Ice cream, cake and custard, soup, mousse, yoghurt, fruit juice and milk drinks are ideal. If your child has diarrhoea, it might be wise to avoid dairy foods for a while. Do not force a sick child to drink or eat; encourage sipping or nibbling throughout the day.

The following conditions, which commonly occur in children, are arranged in alphabetical order for ease of reference.

Allergies to Food

Allergies are adverse reactions to specific substances, such as penicillin or peanuts (see page 106), that the body perceives as foreign.

Allergies

In their most serious form, food allergies are life-threatening, but at their most subtle may be no more than an itchy rash. Whatever form the food allergy takes, determining its causes can be very difficult because the average diet includes such a wide range of foods, many of them processed and containing numerous ingredients. Even when the offending substance is known, it can still be difficult to avoid it, especially at social gatherings, in restaurants or on holiday. Managing a child with a true food allergy requires constant vigilance, and helping a young child to understand why, for example, he can't have chocolate can be very tricky.

Although food allergy is on the increase, it is important to remember that true food allergy is still quite rare.

Paul Sacher's Top Tip
Stop feeding your child immediately if he develops any alarming symptoms after eating a food. Signs to watch for include vomiting, swollen lips or eyes, difficulty breathing or explosive diarrhoea. Seek immediate medical advice following the appearance of any of these symptoms.

Did you know?
Food allergy is diagnosed in 3–7 per cent of children before their third birthday, but it often disappears before adulthood. By five years of age, 98 per cent of children will lose their allergy to eggs and milk. However, allergies to peanuts (see page 106) and tree nuts (almonds, Brazil nuts and hazelnuts) are more likely to persist, and may co-exist with asthma.

There are two types of food allergies: immediate (symptoms appear quickly) and delayed (symptoms appear slowly).

Immediate reactions

Food allergies that provoke an immediate reaction (within two hours) are more life-threatening than those with delayed reactions, but are easier to diagnose and thus pinpoint problem foods. The medical term for a severe allergic reaction is anaphylaxis. Symptoms include flushing of the skin; nettle rash (hives) anywhere on the body; swollen lips, tongue, mouth or throat; difficulty swallowing or speaking; stomach pain, nausea and vomiting; itchy or blistered skin; coughing, wheezing or sneezing; low blood pressure; abnormal heartbeat; collapse and unconsciousness. If you notice any of these symptoms in your child, take him straight to the nearest accident and emergency department. Swollen lips, tongue and throat can cause problems with breathing, which can have devastating consequences.

It is important to identify the offending food so that it can be avoided in the future. Anaphylactic reactions can be treated whatever the cause, provided you get help quickly. If you are unsure what to do, call NHS Direct for advice (see page 204), or go straight to the nearest accident and emergency department.

Did you know?

There is no completely accurate allergy test. The tests most commonly used in hospital allergy clinics are blood tests (RAST, CAP-RAST and ELISA) and skin-prick tests, but even these are not entirely reliable. Other tests often advertised by private allergy clinics, such as hair analysis and electrode tests, have been evaluated in a Consumer Association report and found to be even more inaccurate. They failed to pick up known allergies in people, and also exaggerated the number of allergies they had, leading to unnecessarily restricted and possibly deficient diets. The report suggested that these types of test are a waste of money.

Delayed reactions

Delayed allergic reactions can cause a wide spectrum of symptoms that may appear up to three days later. Symptoms include reflux (see page 187), stomach pain or bloating; poor growth; diarrhoea or constipation; eczema and asthma. Such allergies are harder to diagnose because of the delayed appearance of symptoms.

Most common foods causing allergies

Known medically as 'allergens', the most common foods implicated in food allergy are milk, wheat, fish and shellfish, egg, soya, peanuts (see page 106) and tree nuts.

Food allergies are hereditary, and your child is much more likely to have one if there is a family history of allergy. This includes eczema, hay fever and asthma, as well as food allergies.

The most accurate way to diagnose food allergy is to avoid the food for six weeks, then to reintroduce it and note any recurrence of symptoms. However, *never* eliminate food groups from your child's diet without the advice of a dietitian.

Egg allergy

To avoid adverse reactions, make sure the following words do not appear on the packaging of any food you buy: egg, egg yolk, egg white, albumin.

Fish and shellfish allergy

Adverse reactions to fish and shellfish can be very severe, so the solution is to avoid these foods entirely. While this is easy to do at home, it can be difficult when eating out because cross-contamination might occur. For example, the same chopping board might be used for meat and fish, or stocks might contain fish ingredients. For this reason, those allergic to fish and shellfish are advised not to eat in restaurants that have these foods on the menu.

Food colourings and preservatives

In 1975 Ben Feingold, an American allergist researching a possible connection between food and behaviour, claimed that hyperactive children could benefit from a diet free of colourings and preservatives. In fact, only a few children responded to the removal of food additives from their diet. Further studies have been inconclusive, but it seems that the behaviour of some children could be affected by food additives. Always consult a paediatric dietitian before putting your child on a restricted diet.

Gluten allergy
An allergy to gluten (the protein in cereals) is known as coeliac disease. If your child is diagnosed with this condition, he will need to follow a gluten-free diet under medical supervision.

Milk allergy
Once you know your child has a milk allergy, always check that the following items are not in the ingredients list of every food you buy: milk, butter, cheese, cream, ghee, yoghurt, casein, caseinates, whey, lactose and milk solids.

If infant formulas based on cow's milk are avoided in infants under one year of age, it is very important to replace them with an extensively hydrolysed formula (see page 6). Do not give infant soya milks to children under six months of age (see page 5), and do not use any other animal milks, as your child may become allergic to these too. Consult a paediatric dietitian to make sure that your allergic child's diet is safe and adequate.

Some children over the age of one may continue on milks prescribed by the doctor; others might prefer suitable alternatives from the supermarket, such as milks made from soya, rice, oats or nuts. These usually taste better than hydrolysed formulas, but their levels of nutrients tend to be lower. To supplement these you could also try offering milk-free desserts and yoghurts, which are both tasty and nutritious. Always make sure your child's milk contains calcium; if not, he must take a calcium supplement.

Peanut and tree-nut allergy
Allergy to peanuts (see page 106) is particularly serious as it appears early in life, is often severe and persists into adulthood. It is recommended that children from allergic families should not have peanuts or peanut products until at least three years of age.

The incidence of allergy to peanuts and tree nuts is increasing, and approximately 1.3 per cent of British children under four years old are allergic to these foods. Peanuts account for the majority of anaphylactic reactions, which can be life-threatening.

Refined peanut oil, as found in many manufactured foods, is safe for most people with peanut allergies, but crude peanut oil should be avoided. If in doubt, avoid the food.

Read labels carefully to see if food products contain nuts. Where this is not possible, such as in restaurants and catering outlets, ask the staff if products contain nuts. If they are not guaranteed nut-free, avoid them.

Soya allergy

If you have identified a soya allergy, check that the following words do not appear on the packaging: hydrolysed/spun/textured vegetable protein, soya flour, soya grits, soy protein isolates, soy sauce, miso, tempeh and tofu. Some children will also have to avoid soya lecithin and soya oil.

Wheat allergy

To ensure that the products you buy are free from wheat, check that the following words do not appear in the ingredients list: wheat flour, rye flour, bulgar wheat, wheat starch, edible bran, modified starch, rusk, batter, breadcrumbs, thickener (unless from a non-wheat or non-rye source). Note that rye products are excluded because rye is often contaminated with wheat.

Prevention of food allergy

It is recommended that babies be exclusively breast-fed (no solids) for the first six months of life to avoid developing a food allergy. This is especially important for infants from allergic families. For these babies, delay weaning until six months (26 weeks) of age and always introduce foods containing soya, fish, wheat and gluten, citrus fruits, eggs and cow's milk one at a time over 2–3 days to determine if that food causes any allergic reaction or discomfort.

As your baby will be getting all his nutrition from you, it is important to have a balanced diet that keeps both of you healthy. Make sure you eat from all the food groups (see Chapters 1 and 2). Note, however, that some very sensitive or allergic babies may be adversely affected by the protein you eat passing to them through your breast milk. If you notice any signs that your baby is uncomfortable after breast-feeding, make a note of the foods you have eaten and see if there is a pattern. If you think a particular food might be causing a problem, try to cut it out of your diet and see if things improve. Make sure, however, that you replace the lost nutrients and energy with other foods. Speak to your health visitor or state-registered dietitian if you need further advice.

If you are unable to breast-feed your allergic baby, you can use special infant formulas, generally prescribed by a GP. Soya formulas should be avoided as there is some question of their safety in young children (see page 5). There is no evidence after six months that, if your child is free of symptoms, any special measures need to be taken or any specific foods need to be avoided when weaning. However, some parents may wish to delay introducing food that can be highly allergenic, for a few more months.

Treatment of allergies

The principal treatment for all food allergies is strict avoidance of the responsible foods (if known). Remember that not all the symptoms of delayed reactions are necessarily related to food. Asthma and eczema, for example, might be triggered by pollen or house-dust mites. Treatment will depend on the type of reaction or symptoms present; asthma might be treated with an inhaler, and eczema with cream.

Symptoms of immediate reactions may get worse every time the allergen is eaten or encountered. In this case, your child might be prescribed adrenaline for use in an emergency. Your GP or paediatrician will show you how to administer the injection. It is worth leaving spare adrenaline treatments with any other carers your child has in case he suffers a reaction when you are not present. For further information contact the Anaphylaxis Campaign (see page 203).

Probiotics

Foods that are probiotic (meaning 'for life') contain live bacteria that have positive effects on our health. These are available in various 'live' forms in drinks and yoghurts, or in dried forms as powders and capsules. Their use in the prevention or treatment of allergies is currently being investigated. One promising result has shown that mothers given a probiotic during the last month of pregnancy, and babies given a probiotic during the first six months of life, have shown improvements in eczema. The problem arises in choosing the right probiotic because there are many different strains of bacteria in the intestines and it's not yet clear which are most useful for particular conditions. Those most commonly used are *Lactobacillus* and *Bifidobacterium*. If you do give your child a probiotic, make sure you give it at the recommended dosage.

Anaemia

Anaemia is a deficiency of red blood cells. Although it may have a number of causes, the most common among children is lack of iron, so that is what we deal with here.

Iron helps us to make healthy red blood cells that carry oxygen around the body. Unfortunately, lack of iron is the most common deficiency in the UK, and is found in about 12 per cent of children between 18 and 29 months. Children from Asian families seem to be at particular risk.

The symptoms of iron deficiency anaemia include poor appetite, tiredness, lethargy and even fractious behaviour – all because there is too little oxygen in the blood. Babies and children who are anaemic tend to cry a lot, are clingy, difficult to rationalise with, may have temper tantrums, are generally run-down and prone to infections. You may also notice that their skin, tongue, nail beds and inner eyelids are very pale, clear signs that the blood is lacking red cells. School-age children may have poor concentration and perform below their potential abilities. Children who are borderline anaemic may not show any of these symptoms until the condition deteriorates.

Iron deficiency anaemia is most commonly caused by not eating enough iron-rich foods. Diets lacking iron, particularly poor vegetarian diets during pregnancy, predispose infants to anaemia. However, full-term babies are born with good stores of iron that last until they are six months of age. At that point it is very important to start weaning exclusively breast-fed babies and introduce iron-rich foods. Formula milks tend to have higher levels of iron, but it is nonetheless important to get your child on to iron-rich solids (see page 87).

Another common cause of iron deficiency anaemia arises from drinking excessive cow's milk. This is because cow's milk is low in iron, and what it does contain is poorly absorbed. After the age of one, do not give your child more than 500ml (17oz) of milk to drink per day, or more than 350ml (12oz) after the age of two. Apart from lacking iron, it will fill children up and replace more nutritious iron-containing foods in the diet.

The good news is that iron deficiency anaemia is easily diagnosed by taking a blood sample and checking the red cell count. If anaemia is present, an iron supplement will be prescribed, which needs to be taken daily for a few months. During that time the diet should also be improved to include more iron-rich foods (see page 38). Note that iron supplements can cause black stools and constipation. To avoid the latter, introduce more foods containing fibre (see page 29) and make sure your child has plenty of fluids.

Colic

Q What is colic and how do I treat it?

A There is no medical consensus on what colic actually is, or what causes it. Babies who cry excessively and for no apparent reason, appearing inconsolable and even in pain, are often said to have colic. It most commonly occurs in babies aged between three weeks and three months, and its incidence has been put at 30–40 per cent, depending on what criteria are used to diagnose it.

Colic is not directly related to your child's diet, but it has been suggested that breast-fed babies can react to foods eaten by their mothers. If you are breast-feeding, try eliminating various foods one at a time and seeing if your baby becomes more settled. As dairy products are the most common cause of allergy in children, try eliminating these first. Be aware, however, that if you eliminate dairy from the diet, you will need to replace it with a calcium supplement and additional energy from other foods.

The vagueness about what causes colic means that there is no reliable treatment for it. Various over-the-counter 'remedies' are available, but there is little evidence that these are effective. However, there are various things you can try to help settle your baby and make things more bearable. Some babies are soothed by being carried around, others prefer to lie in their cots and be gently massaged, and some can settle only when certain music is played repeatedly. All babies are unique, so experiment to discover what works for your child. Most babies outgrow colic by about three months with no harmful consequences.

Other things to try

- Massage helps to reduce pain and tension in your baby's body, and is also quite relaxing for the parent. Use baby oil or lotion, a little vegetable oil, or some diluted essential oil, as mentioned opposite.

- Soothing sounds, such as rolling waves, nursery rhymes, lullabies can all have a soothing effect.

- Movement might help to soothe your child, or distract him from the pain. Try holding your baby in different positions while rocking him.

If nothing seems to help your baby, and he is still crying a lot and appears to be in pain, he may be suffering from reflux (see page 187).

Gina Ford's Top Tip

When a baby has a tendency to suffer colic, I would first check if the colic is being caused by the mother's diet (see page 166). If this is not the case, I would then check if the colic is being caused by either hunger in the early evening or overtiredness. Often a breast-feeding mother can be very tired towards the early evening and this can result in a low milk supply. I would therefore suggest that the mother tries topping her baby up with a formula feed at this time to see if this improves the situation. Otherwise, overtiredness could be the cause of excessive crying. It is very important to ensure that a baby under three months is never allowed to stay awake for longer than one and a half to two hours. If neither hunger nor over-tiredness appear to be affecting your baby then the next most common cause of excessive crying or colic is overfeeding. If you feed your baby on demand this can often lead to a baby having another feed before the first one has been digested. If I thought this were the case then, depending on the age, the symptoms of the baby, and how often he is feeding throughout the evening and the middle of the night, I would introduce dilute sugar water. With a baby between one and three months of age, who is feeding excessively in the night and consistently putting on more than the recommended weight gain each week, I would try to replace one of the night feeds with some dilute sugar water. When the baby wakes in the night I would give 120ml (4oz) of cool, boiled water mixed with half a teaspoon of sugar to settle him. At this stage I find plain boiled water does not have the same effect. The following day I would wake the baby at 7am, regardless of how little sleep he has had in the night, and then proceed with the *Contented Little Baby* routine throughout the day to 6.30pm. At this time I would always offer a breast-fed baby a top-up of expressed milk to ensure that he has had enough to drink. This avoids him needing to feed again in two hours, which is a common pattern in babies suffering from colic. With a bottle-fed baby, I always make sure that the 2.30pm feed is small so that he feeds well at 6.30pm.

With an older baby of three months or more, I would attempt to eliminate middle-of-the-night feeds altogether, or at least reduce them to only one. It is important to ensure that the baby feeds well at 6.30pm, if necessary offering a top-up of expressed milk at this time. I believe that a low milk supply early evening is often the cause of a baby feeding little and often, which can lead to him not digesting feeds properly.

More often than not, the baby settles well the first night, but occasionally a baby may have developed the wrong sleep associations as a result of the colic. With these babies I use the controlled crying method of sleep training, and within 3–4 nights they are going down happily and sleeping well until the 10.30pm feed. As they have slept well and have gone a full four hours since their last feed, they feed well and will go on to last for an even longer spell in the night. Depending on their age, they are given either a feed or sugar water. A baby of three months or older who is capable of going from the last feed through to 6am or 7am should be given sugar water for a week. Gradually reduce the amount of sugar until he is taking plain water.

This method, along with the routines, will encourage a baby who has suffered from colic and developed the wrong sleep associations to sleep through the night, normally within a couple of weeks. I cannot stress enough that the success depends on the use of the sugar water during the first week. I am not sure why it works; it is a tip I picked up from an older maternity nurse over 25 years ago and it has never failed. Parents are often concerned that it will encourage babies to develop a sweet tooth. As the sugar water is used for such a short period, I have never seen any problem.

Constipation

In simple terms, constipation is the inability to empty the bowel frequently and/or easily. It affects 1–3 per cent of children, often making them feel uncomfortable, listless and irritable. It can also reduce appetite, which decreases the intake of food and fluid, making the problem worse. Sometimes there is pain on passing stools and occasionally bleeding from the bottom. This can make children fearful of having bowel movements.

Average stool frequency in children has been estimated at about four stools per day in the first week of life, reducing to about two per day between the ages of one and two. By the age of four a child will have between three per day and three per week, which goes to show that there is a lot of variation in normal bowel habits. Investigation is required only if a child experiences abnormal symptoms or discomfort when going to the toilet.

If you are concerned, ask your child not to flush the toilet after a bowel movement so that you can look for any evidence of hard stools, pellet-like stools or fresh blood. This will help your doctor to make a diagnosis. Laxatives, generally in syrup form, are often prescribed for children, and these help to get things moving. In some cases, if the constipation is particularly bad, a suppository may be prescribed. Once your child's constipation has improved, slowly increase the fibre in the diet and reduce the dose of laxative (as recommended by your GP).

Signs that your child might be constipated

- Poor appetite; being constipated can lead to a bloated abdomen that makes the child feel full and not very hungry.

- Bowels open less than three times per week.

- Strain when passing stool.

- Reluctance to go to the toilet for fear of passing a hard stool.

- Complains of stomach pain, or pain when passing stool.

- Fresh red blood in the stool.

- Soils clothes rather than using the toilet.

The importance of fibre

More often than not, constipation is caused by poor diet, particularly a lack of fibre. Diets full of processed foods are usually low in fibre and high in fat, which can slow down the rate at which foods move from the stomach through the digestive system. Fibre is not absorbed like the rest of the food we eat: it passes through the digestive system unchanged, acting like a broom and helping to sweep everything through the gut and keeping it running smoothly.

Fibre is found in cereals, fruits, vegetables and nuts (see page 29). Unfortunately, many children do not eat fruit and vegetables or anything unrefined, such as wholegrain bread. The modern habit of grazing rather than eating proper meals probably also plays a part in the development of constipation because there is nothing bulky enough to encourage movement through the intestine. In addition, some children drink excessive amounts of milk, which does not contain any fibre and therefore exacerbates the problem.

If you have a child with constipation, encourage the whole family to eat more high-fibre foods and your child will not feel like the odd one out.

Paul Sacher's Top Tip

Fluid intake is very important in avoiding constipation. Refer to the fluid intake chart (see page 53) to make sure your child is drinking enough. Fibre absorbs water as it passes through the digestive system, making the stools softer and easier to pass.

High-fibre foods
Try to include one food from this list at each meal.

- Wholegrain cereal, e.g. Weetabix, Shredded Wheat, porridge, muesli.

- Wholemeal, granary or rye bread, or white bread with added fibre; wholemeal pitta bread, chapattis, scones, muffins and crumpets.

- Wholemeal flour; when baking, replace half the white flour with wholemeal.

- Oatcakes, digestive biscuits, cereal bars and flapjacks.

- Wholemeal pasta.

- Brown rice.

- Fruit – but make sure you leave the skin on (if edible) and wash it thoroughly. Include dried fruit, e.g. a box of raisins or a handful of apricots, in packed lunches.

- Vegetables – lightly cooked; leave the skin on potatoes to maximise their fibre content. Serve raw vegetables, e.g. carrots, baby sweetcorn, mangetout, with dips, e.g. hummus, tzatziki or guacamole.

- Pulses, e.g. baked beans, peas and lentils.

- Nuts – only for children aged five upwards because of the risk of choking (see page 106).

Note: Unprocessed bran should not be given to children because it can cause blockage of the intestinal tract and also prevent absorption of minerals from food.

Compromise for success

Don't try to change your child's diet overnight. Introduce changes gradually so that the new eating habits become established for life and will keep constipation at bay forever. To achieve your goal, compromise will often be necessary, for example:

- Make sandwiches with one slice of white bread and one slice of wholemeal bread.

- Mix your child's favourite cereal with a fibre-containing one, e.g. cornflakes plus muesli. (Breakfast is a very important meal and helps to get things moving.)

- Stir a little dried fruit, e.g. raisins, sultanas, chopped prunes or figs, into flavoured yoghurt or fromage frais.

- Mix baked beans, butter beans or sweetcorn into favourite dishes, such as cottage pie or meatloaf.

- Offer dried fruit, muesli bars or high-fibre cereal bars instead of crisps and sweets.

Cutting down on snacks and eating regular meals will help to create the desire to pass stool. Try also to establish routines for going to the toilet at a certain time each day.

Finally, do not feel that you have failed if, despite all efforts, laxatives are still required. It is important to keep up the fibre content in the diet to minimise the amount of laxative needed.

Constipated babies

If your baby is constipated, make sure he is having sufficient fluid and that, if bottle-fed, you are making up the feeds with the correct amount of water. Also make sure that you include some fibrous foods in his weaning diet. Babies who are formula-fed are more likely to have hard stools than those who are breast-fed. This is thought to be due to the difference in the digestion of the fat in the milk and also the different absorption rates.

It has been suggested that formulas based on whey may be preferable to those based on casein. If your baby is suffering from constipation that is not getting any better, it may be related to a food allergy or problem with the digestive system, so consult your GP.

Ideas for increasing fibre in your baby's diet

- Serve high-fibre cereals, such as wheat biscuits and oats, for breakfast.

- Puréed, stewed fruit makes a tasty weaning food that is full of fibre. Add prunes for their laxative effect.

- Include vegetables or fruit at each meal.

- Ensure your baby is taking enough fluid (see page 53).

- Offer diluted prune juice (1:5 with water) as a drink, but not more than 50–120ml (2–4oz) a day.

Natalie, aged 12 weeks

Problem: Constipation

Cause: Premature transition from breast milk to over-rich infant formula

Natalie weighed just over 3.6kg (8lb) at birth and was exclusively breast-fed for the first six weeks. She regained her birth weight within nine days and continued to gain weight well each week, weighing a healthy 4.8kg (10lb 5oz) at six weeks of age. She was also sleeping well from her last feed at 10pm right through until 6.30am. Her mother, Lindsey, who was self-employed, planned to return to work part-time for four days a week when Natalie was eight weeks old, so she decided to introduce one formula feed at 10pm when Natalie was just over six weeks. This meant that the milk she expressed at 10pm, along with milk she would express at work, could be used for the mid-morning feed and mid-afternoon feed on the days she was at work.

Natalie adapted easily to her new routine of being part breast-fed and part bottle-fed. She would easily drink 210–240ml (7–8oz) of expressed milk on the days that Lindsey was at work, and continued to be a happy, easy baby until she reached nine weeks. She then went through a growth spurt and started to demand feeds sooner than she used to, often taking a full 270ml (9oz) feed and screaming for more. Lindsey began to find it more and more difficult to express enough milk to meet Natalie's increased demands, and a sudden bout of very serious gastroenteritis resulted in Lindsey being admitted to hospital for several days. She became very weak and her milk supply reduced dramatically because of her illness. Natalie's increased demands for milk had to be met by giving her more formula milk during the day.

By the time Lindsey left hospital, Natalie, who was then aged nine weeks, was down to having only two breast-feeds a day, and taking 210–270ml (7–9oz) of formula at all her other feeds. She was no longer as happy and contented, and would get very upset when straining to do a poo. By the time she reached 11 weeks, she was doing a poo only every 2–3 days, was irritable for much of her waking time, and had also started to wake up much earlier in the morning. Well-meaning relations convinced Lindsey that Natalie was a hungry baby, that breast milk was not satisfying her, and that hunger was the reason for her doing a poo only every few days. By the time Natalie reached 12 weeks, Lindsey had abandoned the remaining two breast-feeds and Natalie was being totally formula-fed. But she still remained irritable and was becoming very constipated.

In desperation, and convinced by family and friends that hunger was the cause, Lindsey transferred Natalie onto a casein-dominant milk which is marketed as suitable for hungrier babies. While she did start to go slightly longer between feeds, she continued to be irritable most of the time and became hysterical when straining to pass a poo. More often than not, this would consist of several hard pellets.

It was at this stage that Lindsey telephoned me for advice on weaning Natalie. She was convinced that Natalie was a hungry baby and that it was hunger causing her to be so irritable and do a poo only every few days.

Natalie now weighed around 6.3kg (14lb) and was drinking 1200–1350ml (40–43oz) of milk a day. This is considerably more than the amount recommended in the fluid table (see page 53). Since Natalie had been such a happy baby until the time she started getting more formula, I was not convinced that hunger was the cause of the problem. It was also far too early to consider weaning Natalie, as she was only 12 weeks old and the minimum recommended age is 26 weeks. I suspected that the main cause of the problem was constipation caused by over-feeding of formula milk.

I explained to Lindsey that I believed things had started to go wrong when Natalie's bottles of expressed milk were suddenly replaced by formula milk. The composition of formula is quite different from breast milk and this is particularly so when expressed breast milk is given from a bottle. A feed of expressed milk usually contains less hind milk, which is 3–5 times fattier than fore milk, so the baby will tend to drink more milk per feed. Breast milk is normally digested more quickly than formula milk, so I usually find that a baby switched from expressed milk in a bottle to a formula feed will drink slightly less formula than he did of breast milk.

This did not happen in Natalie's case, but I believe the reason for that was her mother's unexpected admittance to hospital. Natalie suddenly had to have all her feeds from a bottle, and the dramatic loss of the physical bond of breast-feeding led to her irritability. Her grandparents assumed that her unhappy mood and excessive crying were due to hunger, and kept offering her more milk each time she cried. Her digestive system had suddenly to cope with more formula-feeds during the day and led to her becoming constipated and even more irritable. The cries of discomfort were misinterpreted for hunger and she was given yet more formula. When Natalie was transferred onto a casein-dominant milk the problem became even more severe, as this milk takes much longer to digest than whey-dominant formula milk.

When a baby is suddenly switched from virtually all breast-feeds to nearly all formula-feeds, constipation can become a real problem, particularly if the baby is not given extra fluids in the way of cool, boiled water until his system gets used to digesting the formula.

Instead of increasing the amount that Natalie took at each feed when she was transferred to bottles of formula, she should have been given slightly less and the additional volume made up with additional water feeds.

I advised that Natalie should be put back onto whey-dominant formula milk and given 180–210ml (6–7oz) at all her daytime feeds, and no more than 210–240ml (7–8oz) at the 6pm and 10pm feeds when she slept longer between feeds. This reduced her daily intake from around 1200–1350ml (40–45oz) a day to approximately 1050–1110ml (35–37oz) a day, which was nearer the recommended amount for her weight.

I also advised that she be offered 30–60ml (1–2 oz) of cool, boiled water between each of her daytime feeds and if she woke around 5am, as this would help her constipation and allow her system to get used to digesting the formula.

Within 10 days, Natalie was back to being a happy, contented baby and having a poo once or twice a day. I then advised her parents that they could now reduce the amount of water that Natalie was being given between feeds to only once or twice a day. If she showed signs of needing slightly extra at some feeds during a growth spurt, they could then increase two of her feeds. Once she was digesting the extra milk at two of the feeds, they could offer extra milk at her other feeds, ensuring that her milk intake was increased according to her growth spurts.

Natalie did continue to wake up slightly earlier than she had previously, but on most occasions she would settle back until 7am, when given a small amount of cool, boiled water. On the mornings she did not settle back within 20 minutes I advised her parents to follow up the cool, boiled water with a few ounces from her first morning bottle. Although her parents were disappointed that Natalie was no longer sleeping through the night as long as she had done before going onto formula, they realised that it was unfair to overfeed her or give an alternative milk and upset her digestive system just for the sake of getting an extra hour's sleep. By the time Natalie was just over four months old, she was sleeping through from 7.15pm until 7am.

Natalie's problem was an extreme case of constipation caused by suddenly overfeeding a digestive system that was used to breast milk. It is very important not to misunderstand the signals when a breast-fed baby is transferred from breast-feeding to formula. Irritability is often caused because the baby is actually missing the physical comfort of sucking from the breast, particularly if it happens suddenly, as when Lindsey had to go into hospital. It is also important to ensure that a baby is offered extra cool, boiled water between feeds until his body is used to digesting formula easily and he is passing a bowel movement every day. I do not believe that it is normal for babies to go several days without a bowel movement. In my experience this always leads to them becoming very uncomfortable and distressed. Ideally, the introduction of formula should always be done gradually, starting with a first-stage formula, the composition of which is much nearer to breast milk than that of milk for hungrier babies.

Diarrhoea

Diarrhoea is the frequent passing of loose stools, and can make changing nappies quite distressing. The most common cause of diarrhoea in children is gastroenteritis (see Vomiting, page 187) which is an intestinal infection that should be treated by a doctor. However, loose stools may be normal in some babies – they're not always a sign of ill health. Generally, more than three loose stools per day is defined as diarrhoea.

Breast-fed babies may have loose stools for the first few weeks of life, which can number 10–12 per day. In some babies this can continue until solids are introduced. The colour of stool also varies, and may even be green in bottle-fed babies. When formula or solids are introduced, the stools become firmer in consistency.

If your child has been prescribed antibiotics to treat an infection, they too can cause diarrhoea, and it may take a while for his stools to return to normal. A course of probiotics (good bacteria) may speed up this process (see page 157 Allergies to Food).

When to worry about diarrhoea

If your child has diarrhoea, but has no other symptoms of illness and is feeding normally, there is probably nothing to be concerned about. If he is vomiting as well and not keeping anything down, seek medical advice straight away because there is a risk of dehydration. In severe cases, fluids may have to be given by a drip in a hospital.

If the diarrhoea persists for more than few days and your child is showing other symptoms, such as a raised temperature (38.0°C and above), poor growth or blood in his stool, seek medical advice immediately.

Q **What dietary treatment is available for diarrhoea?**

A There is no specific dietary treatment for diarrhoea. Breast-feeding or formula-feeding should not be interrupted except on medical advice. Do not give soft drinks (commercial or home-made), sweetened fruit drinks, sweetened tea, coffee or medicinal teas and infusions because these can make the diarrhoea worse. Food should not be restricted, as this could cause weight loss, but fatty and sugary foods should be avoided until the diarrhoea settles.

Changing the diet might help in specific conditions, such as diarrhoea related to food allergy (see page 160). After long periods of diarrhoea, some children might develop a condition called secondary lactose intolerance, which means that they are unable to break down the sugar in milk. This can cause further diarrhoea, bloating, stomach pain and lots of wind. The treatment for this depends on the age of the child.

- Under one year – try using a lactose-free infant formula, available from pharmacies.
- Over one year – introduce soya milk products, which are lactose free, and make sure they are fortified with calcium.

After long periods of diarrhoea, levels of good bacteria in the intestine may be low, so it might be worth giving your child a course of probiotics to help restore levels to normal (see page 164).

Excess Weight and Obesity

In the UK, one in five children is overweight and one in 10 is obese. In fact, excess weight among children is currently the most serious child health-care issue and on the increase in most Western countries of the world.

Q **How can I tell if my child is overweight?**

A It can be very difficult to tell whether babies or children are overweight just by looking at them. Some families are genetically bigger than others, and some children appear large for their age and will end up being large adults. An objective way to tell if a child is becoming overweight or not is to continue plotting his weight and height regularly on the growth chart in his red book (see page 66). If the weight measurements begin to outstrip the height measurements and start to cross lines upwards, this may be a sign that he is gaining excessive weight. In this case, speak to your GP or other trained health professional.

Social aspects of obesity

The current thinking is that the epidemic of obesity is an environmental problem and that it is no longer acceptable to blame individuals. The society we live in encourages inactivity and constantly promotes convenience foods that are high in fat, sugar and salt. While there may be some truth in thinking that individuals are not wholly to blame, the fact remains that excess weight has serious repercussions on health, and brings other problems in its wake. Overweight children are often bullied and teased at school, and may become depressed, which impacts on the whole family.

Healthy eating habits start early, and even the youngest of children will quickly pick up good and bad habits from those around them. For example, there is no point telling a two-year-old to eat his vegetables when you don't eat any yourself. Set a good example for children by eating healthily yourself.

The other important factor in becoming overweight is lack of exercise. Parents have only to compare their own childhood habits with those of the present generation to see how sedentary life has become. The average child now spends up to six hours a day watching television or playing computer games. Fear of crime also keeps children indoors or means they are ferried about in cars.

Did you know?
Consumption of soft drinks has increased by almost 500 per cent over the last 50 years, and they are now the largest source of added sugars in the diet.

What you can do

- Breast-feed your baby. Breast-feeding is associated with lower levels of childhood obesity.

- Encourage healthy eating with three meals a day and a couple of healthy snacks, such as fruit, yoghurt or low-fat cheese.

- Make sure your child has a good breakfast, as this has been shown to lead to decreased snacking in the morning and higher achievement at school.

- Increase physical activity to help children maintain a healthy weight. Do fun things as a family that involve being active, e.g. cycling, football and swimming.

- Use low-fat products for children over five and read the labels to ensure the fat hasn't been replaced with sugar.

- Offer your child milk or water rather than sugary drinks.

- Allow only 150ml (5oz) of fruit juice per day. This counts as one of the recommended five daily portions of fruit and vegetables, but is naturally high in sugar, so should not be allowed freely in the diet.

- Grill, boil or bake foods without added fat, rather than frying.

- Avoid take-away or convenience foods, as these are often very high in calories.

- Walk your child to school at least a couple of times a week.

- Restrict the amount of time your children spend watching TV or playing computer games.

- Do not allow children to eat in front of the television.

- Set a good example. Most children learn food choices and habits from their parents, especially their mothers.

- Implement regular family meals.

- Do not allow children to 'graze' or snack continually throughout the day.

- Reduce children's access to high-calorie foods.

- Offer children smaller portions and do not allow them second helpings.

- Include your children in the planning and preparing of healthy, balanced meals. Make food preparation fun, and include items they enjoy. This is also a good time to introduce foods they have previously refused or not tried before. By including children in the preparation, they are much more likely to try new tastes.

- Do not label foods as good or bad, or use food as rewards or treats; you will only make the 'bad' ones more tempting.

- Allow your child to make his own judgement about how much he should eat. Children's appetites vary widely from day to day, and parents who excessively control their intake leave them poorly equipped to regulate their own appetites.

Exercise for children aged 2–6 years

- Adventure playgrounds are lots of fun and encourage social interaction with other children. Find out what recreational facilities for young children are available in your area.

- Climbing frames are great for improving balance and strength.

- Swimming, diving and playing games in a pool are great energy burners; they are also very safe forms of activity as there is no weight bearing on growing bones. Find out where your nearest public pool is and whether they have swimming lessons for young children.

- Encourage your child to play outdoor games, such as 'tag', or indoor games, such as musical chairs, if the weather is bad. Chasing games are fun and they increase the heart rate.

- Walk with your child whenever possible instead of using the car. Park a few roads away from your destination and slowly build up the amount of time you and your child spend walking.

Poor Growth

Children and babies can fail to grow well for many different reasons. Sometimes the causes are medical, sometimes behavioural, such as fussy eaters refusing food, and sometimes inexplicable. Poor growth can be diagnosed only by having your child regularly measured and weighed, and the results plotted on the growth chart in his child health care record (red book). Depending on the severity of the poor growth, medical and or dietary action may be required.

Q What is poor growth?

A When a child grows less well than the averages established on the growth charts, he is said to be suffering from poor growth. It is not unusual for children to go through periods of poor growth, perhaps because of illness or fussy eating, and most quickly bounce back. For some, however, poor growth can lead to a more serious condition known as faltering growth, which requires medical intervention. Both poor growth and faltering growth can only be diagnosed by having your child's weight and height measured regularly by health professionals. You should be concerned in the following situations and seek medical advice:

- If your child's weight or height measurements start flattening out on the growth chart (see page 66) and crossing the centile lines downwards.
- If there is a difference of more than two centiles (lines) between his weight and height.
- If your child's weight or height falls below the bottom line on the centile chart.

Q What causes poor growth?

A There are many reasons for poor growth, including the following:

- Behavioural problems, such as refusing to eat enough food or the right types of food.
- Inadequate parenting skills can lead to poor growth. Young parents may not have learnt to cook for themselves, let alone for a young child.
- Lack of cooking facilities, such as stoves, microwaves and kettles, make it difficult to prepare nutritious food for babies.
- Inadequate surfaces and poor hygiene can lead to the baby suffering from increased infections, which can cause poor growth.

Poor growth and faltering growth are symptoms of illness rather than illnesses themselves. When children are unwell, especially with a high temperature, they lose their appetite, which, over prolonged periods, can lead to weight loss and poor growth. Other medical conditions, such as constipation and reflux (see pages 167 and 187) can also lead to poor growth. Any child not growing well should have a thorough medical examination to determine the underlying cause. If none can be discovered, use the advice below to boost your child's energy intake and promote better growth.

> **Did you know?**
> Faltering growth affects about 5 per cent of all children in the UK, and is most common in the under-twos.

What you can do

If your child is growing poorly, use the following tips (devised by dietitians at Great Ormond Street Hospital for Children) to increase the energy in his diet and promote better growth. Note that this advice is only for children who are growing poorly. It is not suitable for any other children, as it could cause excessive weight gain, leading to obesity.

- Encourage your child to eat a variety of foods, and try increasing the calories in his food and drinks.

- Increase the amount of food your child is eating, but do not force him or make a big issue of it. Try offering more frequent snacks or puddings after meals.

- Use full-fat milk at breakfast time, and when making soups, sauces, mashed potato and drinks.

- Encourage milky drinks made with full-fat milk and flavoured with drinking chocolate, milkshake powder or syrup.

- Offer dessert pots, such as full-fat yoghurt, rice pudding or fromage frais, after meals or as a snack in between.

- Serve full-fat yoghurt with chopped-up fruit, or blend together to make a smoothie.

- Use full-fat cheeses and spreads; hard cheeses, such as Cheddar, are usually higher in fat than soft ones.

- Add grated cheeses to sauces, omelettes, scrambled eggs and pasta dishes. Also sprinkle cheese on to vegetables, baked beans, soups, pizzas and potatoes.

- Offer snacks such as cheese on toast or cheese sandwiches.

- Increase the fat in your child's diet by frying or roasting foods such as meat and fish.

- Do not remove fat from meat, and leave the skin on chicken.

- Choose tuna or sardines in oil rather than in brine or spring water.

- Use hummus as a dip or as a spread on bread or crackers.

- Spread butter or margarine on bread or crackers, and add to jacket and mashed potatoes.

- Melt butter or margarine over foods such as vegetables and rice.

- Add oil dressings or mayonnaise to salad vegetables.

- Add cream to breakfast cereals, porridge, pasta sauces, mashed potato and soup; serve with fruit, jelly, pancakes, scones or cakes; mix into milk and add to milkshakes.

- Offer sugary squash and fizzy drinks (not the diet varieties).

- Spread honey, jam and syrup on bread, or pour over puddings.

- Add sugar to foods such as breakfast cereals, drinks, puddings and hot drinks (remember to brush teeth twice a day). Note that, it is better for teeth to have sugary drinks at mealtimes rather than between meals.

- Use full-fat and sweetened foods rather than low-fat or reduced-sugar products.

High-energy meals should improve growth, but if your child cannot eat large amounts at mealtimes, offer frequent high-energy snacks instead, such as:

- Chocolate

- Crisps and savoury snacks

- Biscuits, especially chocolate, cream-filled or jam-filled varieties

- Crackers with cheese or dips

- Buttered popcorn (a choking hazard, so watch carefully)

- Ice cream

- Dairy dessert snacks, such as chocolate mousse and full-fat yoghurt

- Milkshakes

- Cereal with full-fat milk and cream

- Chocolate spread

- Dried fruit, canned fruit in syrup and fruit bars

Possetting, Reflux and Vomiting

Possetting

Bringing up a small quantity of milk, particularly during winding, is known as possetting, and is a normal occurrence during the first year of life. It is not distressing or uncomfortable to the baby, and does not occur with every feed. It is more common among bottle-fed babies because they tend to take in more air than breast-fed babies when feeding.

Although babies are untroubled by possetting, their parents can feel anxious and inadequate. Changing the baby's clothes – and frequently your own – can make you feel that you must be doing something wrong. In fact, 90 per cent of babies who posset will gradually improve on their own without any medical intervention. In the remaining 10 per cent who posset frequently, it can lead to problems, such as dehydration and irritation (possibly infection) of the oesophagus.

> **Did you know?**
> Approximately 50 per cent of infants regurgitate more than twice a day.

Ideas to prevent possetting

- Give small, more frequent feeds.

- At intervals during feeding, rest your baby in an upright position to allow swallowed air to escape.

- Don't overfeed your baby.

- Raise the head of the cot slightly so that your baby is lying on a gentle incline. Gravity will help the milk move down his digestive system.

- Don't let your baby swallow a lot of air with feeds. To prevent this, make sure the bottle is tilted at the correct angle to allow milk to fill the teat, and remove the bottle when the milk is finished.

- Feed your baby in an upright position, never when he is lying flat. Try to prevent him hunching over in your arms or lap, as this will hamper the movement of milk down his digestive system.

- Support your baby in a sitting position for at least 45 minutes after feeding to bring up the wind.

- Change your baby's nappy before feeding rather than when his stomach is full.

- Handle your baby very gently after feeding: avoid sudden movements, rocking and bouncing, and do not pat him vigorously.

- Never let anyone smoke near your baby. There is some evidence that passive smoking may increase possetting.

- Change the bottle teat to one that allows the flow of milk to be slowed down.

Milk thickeners

There are various over-the-counter and prescription preparations that can be added to infant milks to thicken them and thereby help reduce possetting. Those added to bottle-feeds can become very thick, so you will have to experiment with different teats to keep them free-flowing. It is also possible to get infant formulas that contain a type of starch that thickens when it reaches the stomach, reducing the ease with which milk can be brought up. These formulas are a normal consistency in the bottle and do not require a different teat. They can be prescribed by your GP or bought over the counter.

Thickeners can also be used with breast-fed babies. Simply make up a paste following the manufacturer's guidelines, and feed it to the baby by mouth before putting him on the breast. The breast milk then mixes with the paste in the stomach, causing it to thicken.

Note that some milk thickeners contain calories, increasing the nutritional content of the feed. These should not be given to babies under one year of age unless they have faltering growth. Babies who are growing well should have non-nutritive thickeners. Read the labels, or ask your GP or pharmacist for guidance. Always use milk thickeners under medical supervision.

When to seek medical help

A couple of small possets daily in an infant who is healthy and gaining weight are no cause for concern. However, if things do not seem to be improving, or your baby is getting distressed during feeding and persistently bringing up a considerable proportion of the feed, a medical consultation is recommended. You should see your GP if the following symptoms are present:

- Difficulties breathing, coughing, wheezing, holding breath or chest infections.

- Swallowing difficulties.

- Signs that your baby is dehydrated (tiredness, dry nappies, dark circles around the eyes).

- Poor weight gain, or none at all.

- Blood in the regurgitated food.

- Constant unsettled behaviour, irritability, crying and difficult to feed.

Reflux

The full term for reflux is gastro-oesophageal reflux (GOR). It is caused by a weak spincter (band of muscle) that connects the oesophagus and the stomach. The sphincter should remain closed, opening only to allow milk or solids into the stomach, but in some cases it opens inappropriately and allows the contents of the stomach to regurgitate back up the oesophagus. The regurgitation may go all the way up and cause a vomit, or it can go unnoticed. Since the contents of the stomach are acidic, it causes a burning sensation, similar to 'heartburn' in adults.

Reflux is not a disease in itself, but a symptom of some other disorder or illness, such as a problem with the valve that connects the food pipe and the stomach, or a problem with the digestion or absorption of food. An estimated 20 per cent of babies regurgitate (which appears as possetting or vomiting) during the first year of life. Mild cases often disappear as the baby grows. Moderate cases cause more distress and require some form of medication from your GP. If you are in any doubt about your child's condition, always seek medical advice. Severe reflux is a serious medical problem and needs to be diagnosed and treated by a paediatrician. In extreme cases, surgery can be performed to alleviate the problem.

If you suspect your child may have reflux

- Do not lie your baby flat after meals. Studies have shown that lying a baby in an elevated position at 30 degrees helps to reduce reflux.

- Do not allow your baby to slump in a seat as this causes increased pressure on his stomach. Place him instead in a seat that reclines.

- Make sure your baby is not being overfed. Feed him regularly (6–7 times a day) to avoid him becoming over-hungry and taking excessive quantities of milk.

- Pre-thickened formulas or thickening agents can be used to reduce vomiting, but these should be prescribed and their use explained by a GP or dietitian.

- Some studies have shown that 30–40 per cent of children with reflux, who do not improve on conventional treatment, have a cow's milk protein allergy and improve on a diet that eliminates it. Never try exclusion diets without supervision from a dietitian (see page 148).

- Medications, ranging from antacids to those that change the rate at which the stomach empties, can be helpful but must be prescribed by a GP.

- A pH study, which measures acidity, can be performed to determine if your baby has reflux or not. This involves a hospital stay, during which a probe on the end of a tube is passed up the nostril and down into the oesophagus, where the pH level is measured for 24 hours.

If your baby has reflux but is growing well, the condition is likely to improve as he grows bigger. Just keeping calm can be very reassuring for a distressed, uncomfortable baby, and can go a long way towards improving things. If you suspect that reflux is affecting your child's health, please consult your GP.

Francesca, aged 4½ years

Problem: Bad behaviour at mealtimes

Causes: Suffered from extreme reflux as a baby

Francesca was a very difficult and fussy feeder from birth and would scream on and off throughout each feed, which could take anything up to two hours at a time. Laura, her mother, although determined to breast-feed her for the first six months, gradually started to introduce bottles of formula around the third week. Although Francesca continued to be difficult at feed times, the fact that Laura could share the feeding with her husband and mother helped her to cope with post-natal depression, which set in when Francesca was about eight weeks old.

Laura struggled on with breast-feeding until Francesca was nearly 12 weeks at which stage her post-natal depression became so bad that she had to be admitted to hospital for treatment. On the doctor's advice, and under pressure from her family, along with the fact that she was disliking every minute that Francesca was on the breast, Laura gave up breast-feeding altogether. It was a very difficult decision for her to make because she firmly believed that breast-feeding played a very important part in mother/baby bonding. However, she realised that she was beginning to resent Francesca and that the physical and emotional demands of being attached to a screaming baby for up to eight hours a day were not doing either her or Francesca any good.

Although it also went against her natural instincts and beliefs, Laura agreed to the family paying for a maternity nurse to come and stay for a month to try and get Francesca into a routine and establish happier feeding times. The nurse they hired came highly recommended and specialised in helping mothers who suffered from post-natal depression.

Francesca had never been a sickly baby, so the doctors had dismissed her difficult behaviour while feeding as colic. However, within three days of caring for her, the nurse became convinced that she was actually suffering from reflux. At her parents' insistence, doctors tested Francesca for reflux and the test came back positive. She was suffering from severe reflux and it had reached such a stage that her oesophagus had become ulcerated.

Francesca was on medication until she was nearly eight months old, and although it helped, feeding times could still be tense. When solids were introduced Francesca always had to be entertained and cajoled to eat at meal-times. At four years of age, when her brother Andrew was born, she was still being spoon-fed part of her meals.

It was after the arrival of her baby brother that meal-times became an even bigger problem for Francesca. Andrew was a very calm and contented baby, who took to the breast immediately, but, like all very young babies, his feeds could often last up to an hour or so at a time. Francesca had been used to her parents' undivided atten-tion for nearly five years, so she was not impressed by the arrival of her baby brother and, in particular, by the amount of time that her mother had to devote to feeding him. Andrew was being fed on demand and his feeds would often coincide with Francesca's mealtimes. Francesca was also used to getting lots of attention at mealtimes and did not respond well to being told that she was a big girl and should be able to feed herself. Laura was really enjoying breast-feeding this time around and was determined not to stop so early. In desperation, to try and keep Francesca happy while she was feeding the baby, she would bribe her with biscuits and juice. This, of course, made meal-times even more difficult, as Francesca would not be so interested in her food after having several biscuits and juice an hour or so earlier. Laura then resorted to bribing her with the promise of ice cream and chocolate if she would eat at least some of her food.

Although deep down she realised that she was con-tributing to Francesca's eating problem by doing this, Laura continued to do so, knowing that it would give her the time she needed to feed Andrew. She also consoled herself with the fact that Francesca's teachers at nursery school had reassured her that on the three days a week she had lunch there, she ate everything that was put in front of her.

However, things took a very serious turn for the worse during the summer holidays when Francesca was having all her meals at home. During the first two weeks her eating and her behaviour got dramatically worse. Her diet consisted mainly of spaghetti hoops, baked beans, oven chips and ham sandwiches. In between meals, when she played up or had tantrums, she was given packets of crisps or chocolate biscuits and sweets along with endless amounts of fruit squash.

Things came to a head one day when Laura had two friends around for lunch along with their two children. In the past they had always been sympathetic to Laura's problem, but that day, when Francesca started her usual bad behaviour at lunch, one of the mothers told Laura that she felt she could no longer allow her own child to witness such bad behaviour at mealtimes and that she no longer wished to meet up for lunch until Laura had sorted out Francesca's behaviour. Laura, devastated at this friend's unexpected and sudden departure, turned for sympathy to her other friend. While sympathetic, her other friend admitted to her that many of the parents in their circle of friends did not want their children being influenced by Francesca's bad behaviour and that polite excuses were often being made to avoid lunch dates.

Laura burst into tears and confessed to her friend that things had got so out of hand with Francesca's eating that she just didn't know how to resolve it. When she tried being very strict with Francesca, she had even more tantrums and was even aggressive to Andrew. This caused Laura so much stress that her milk supply would immediately decrease, causing Andrew, who was still feeding on demand, to demand feeding even more often. This led to the unhappy vicious circle of both children demanding more and more from Laura at the same time.

Laura's friend had consulted me when her baby was nine months old and had suddenly started to refuse solids, so she suggested that she should call me to see if I could help. When Laura phoned me we talked at great length about how the situation had come about. Like many parents who have to suffer the anguish and difficulty of feeding a reflux baby, Laura felt very guilty that Francesca's feeding problems in the early days had been caused by something she perhaps had or hadn't done.

In my experience, feeding a baby who suffers from reflux can be a very stressful business, and it can often be difficult to continually love a baby who screams every time you attempt to feed him. While the problem of reflux can disappear altogether, often between the ages of six and nine months, the associations of difficult feeding often continue long afterwards for both the baby and the parents. Once the baby is taking solids, many parents become so anxious for him to eat well that they go to extreme lengths to get him to eat everything that is put in front of him. From the number of calls I receive each month, there is an obvious link between children who suffered reflux as a baby and toddlers and older children who become fussy feeders. I believe that the link is more psychological than physiological.

Bribes of puddings and a sweet if toddlers eat all their meals are nearly always introduced from an early age, as is entertaining at mealtimes, and spoon-feeding continues long after the child is able to feed himself. While this type of bribery works in the short term, I believe that it often leads to real feeding difficulties as the child gets older because he soon learns to use food as a means of getting the parents' attention. This was particularly obvious in Francesca's situation.

Once Andrew was born, Francesca did not get the amount of attention she was used to, particularly at mealtimes. She used the mild forms of bribery that were already in place to her advantage. She quickly realised that she would be given treats if she promised to behave, but also that once she had eaten them there was no further reason to behave. A sure way of getting her mother's attention when Laura was feeding Andrew was to misbehave yet again, despite being given the treat and promising to behave.

Laura agreed that this was exactly how she got into the situation, and she also confessed that a further reason she tended to give in so much to Francesca's demands was that she felt guilty about the fact that she sometimes felt resentful towards her. She had never enjoyed Francesca as a baby because of the feeding problems, and with Andrew it was such a wonderful experience that she resented it when Francesca demanded attention during his feeding times.

The first suggestion I made to Laura was that she should deal with Andrew's erratic feeding times. By putting him into a feeding routine, she would be able to spend more one-to-one time with Francesca at mealtimes. This would help eliminate some of the resentment that she felt towards her baby brother. Once this was established, we could then work at eliminating the problem of all the convenience snack food that Francesca was eating, and the problem of food being used as a bribe for behaving well.

It took Laura nearly two weeks to establish feeding times at 6.45am, 10.45am, 2.30pm, 5pm and 6.30pm for Andrew, who was about six months old by this time. Once fed and changed, he was happy to play under his gym or sit in his chair while Laura ate breakfast with Francesca at 7.30am and tea at 5.30pm. He went down for a nap at 12 noon, so she could also have lunch with Francesca at 12.30pm.

While Francesca was still eating the same restricted diet, the amounts she would eat had increased dramatically because she was no longer being given sweets or biscuits in between meals. Instead of using these treats as a bribe,

I had advised Laura that when Francesca demanded treats in between meals, she was to tell her that she could certainly have a biscuit or an ice cream but they would have one together after they had eaten their lunch. This is where Laura had to be very strong and resist Francesca's tantrums. I advised her not to get into a discussion, simply tell her that she could have a piece of fruit or some raisins, but no biscuits until after lunch.

During the first week of implementing these rules I got several desperate, tearful calls from Laura. She found it very difficult to listen to Francesca screaming and demanding a treat, particularly when she cried, 'I love you, Mummy. I promise to be a good girl if you give me a biscuit.' Laura felt that Francesca's behaviour had improved a lot and that she was being very cruel by not allowing her the occasional little treat, and she feared that Francesca would start to hate her and see her as a cruel and mean mother. I reassured her that this would not be the case as she was not denying Francesca a treat outright, she was simply saying that they would have the treat together after they had eaten their lunch or tea. I explained to Laura that it was important to eliminate completely the use of food as a bribe for good behaviour.

I suggested that she should watch for the signs that Francesca was going to misbehave and prevent a tantrum by doing something interesting with her. When I have had to deal with this problem I have the ingredients on hand to make a jelly or custard trifle (use ready-made in emergencies). The child loves to spend ages mixing everything up, putting it in a bowl and decorating it. I then explain how it has to sit in the fridge for a short while to set but that it will be lovely to eat after we have lunch or tea. This worked wonderfully with Francesca, and on the days that they could not get out to the park or play dates, much time was spent making trifles and little cakes.

It took nearly a month before Francesca stopped making demands for treats, but once a pattern had emerged of regular mealtimes without tantrums, and healthy snacks at the right times, we then dealt with the problem of Francesca eating such a limited variety of foods. I suggested that Laura buy an excellent book called *Easy Peasy* (see page 205), a delightful children's cookery book with excellent pictures and easy step-by-step recipes. I advised Laura to set aside three times a week when Francesca and she could sit down and look at the book and choose a recipe they would cook for a meal that day. They would then go to the shops together and buy the food, then make the meal together. Francesca was very excited about this and insisted on cooking extra for Daddy. She enjoyed making little pizzas with different toppings and mini burgers with tomato sauce. Gradually over the weeks Laura managed to introduce more and more healthy food at mealtimes, using the plan of shopping and cooking together. Laura could also now confidently invite other children around for tea and take Francesca to other children's houses for occasional lunch or tea.

By the time Francesca went back to school full time after the summer holidays, she was eating fish, chicken and beef, plus vegetables such as mini roast potatoes, baby corn, courgettes, carrots, occasional broccoli and roasted peppers on pizzas. Being at school and eating with other children helped Francesca to expand the range of vegetables and fruits she would eat, and learn not always to expect sweet puddings after each meal.

With children of Francesca's age, it is virtually impossible and unrealistic to deny them treats, but biscuits, ice creams and sweets should never be used as a reward for good behaviour or as an incentive to eat healthier food. They should be used in moderation and never as a bribe. There is a fine line between bribery and reward, and very young children need to learn that treats, particularly food treats, come as a result of good behaviour, not something they get to prevent bad behaviour.

Vomiting

Children vomit for various reasons, some medical, some behavioural. Babies who vomit regularly and bring up large amounts of feed should be investigated medically as this could be a sign of reflux (see page 187). Those who vomit a couple of hours after a feed and bring up digested milk or green bile should also be seen by a doctor. In rare cases, vomiting can be caused by an abnormality in the baby's digestive tract, but this is often spotted at birth and dealt with appropriately. A one-off vomit is nothing to worry about as long as your child is otherwise well.

If your baby has a temperature or seems unwell and is vomiting most feeds, he is probably suffering from a virus that causes gastroenteritis, commonly called a 'stomach bug'. Gastroenteritis often occurs in children and can last for 24 hours or up to a few days. The main risk with this is dehydration, as your baby can't keep any fluids down. This may sometimes be compounded by diarrhoea, another common symptom. Stomach bugs are quite contagious, and you will often find that other members of the family suffer some of the same symptoms.

Apart from the risk of dehydration, most children recover from sickness and there are generally no serious long-lasting problems.

Q **What should I do if my child is vomiting?**

A • If your baby is vomiting occasionally and has diarrhoea (frequent, watery stools), continue breast-feeding or feed him his normal infant milk, and offer supplementary sips of water or oral rehydration solution (available from chemists). Oral rehydration solution is a mixture that replaces the minerals lost in watery diarrhoea and decreases the risk of dehydration.

- If your baby is vomiting most feeds and can't keep down even water or oral rehydration solution, consult your GP. In the most severe case, you may need to take your baby to the nearest accident and emergency department, as he may need to be put on a drip to prevent dehydration.

- Do not give babies dairy products, other than breast milk or infant formula, as they can sometimes aggravate a sensitive tummy.

- Continue to offer foods that are plain and bland.

- Offer toddlers and young children pieces of toast with some clear broth and let them feed at their own pace.

Behavioural vomiting

Some vomiting is a learnt behaviour rather than the result of a medical condition. It can, for example, occur in children who had feeding and vomiting problems during their early years. Children who have a history of reflux (see page 187) can also develop behavioural vomiting, as can children who have been force-fed and acquired negative associations about food. Vomiting can be a way of saying 'I don't like this food', or even a way of getting attention.

If you think there is genuine cause for concern, seek medical advice. If, on the other hand, you feel your child is vomiting out of habit rather than for medical reasons, you can try the following:

- Never force-feed a child. A healthy child will not starve himself, so try other ways of feeding, such as offering finger foods and allowing your child to have some control over what he eats.

- If your child vomits, don't make a big fuss. Ignore the incident and wait a while before cleaning up. If you rush straight over, he will associate vomiting with attention and learn to do it more frequently. Praise him for good behaviour and don't get visibly upset or pay him any attention when he vomits.

Poisons

Vomiting can, of course, be caused by food poisoning or accidentally drinking something toxic. Always make sure you keep cooked food separate from raw foods, especially meat, chicken and fish. Any surfaces that these foods have come into contact with should be washed with warm, soapy water or a kitchen disinfectant spray. If your child accidentally swallows a potentially poisonous substance, take him to your nearest accident and emergency department, and always take the substance that was swallowed along with you as this will determine the type of treatment he receives.

Seeking Professional Help

If you are concerned about your child's health and growth, you can call the NHS Direct helpline (see page 204) for free advice from trained nurses. The line is open 24 hours a day, 365 days a year.

If your concern persists, visit your GP or paediatrician for some routine tests and measurements that should reassure you.

The best advice on feeding your child can be obtained from a paediatric dietitian, who is highly trained in the field of children's nutrition. Paediatric dietitians work in conjunction with GP surgeries and community paediatricians, as well as in hospitals that have a children's ward or children's clinics. Waiting lists to see an NHS paediatric dietitian vary from place to place, and urgent referrals are seen sooner than those for more general problems. If you want to avoid the wait, you can obtain a list of dietitians who practise privately by sending a stamped self-addressed envelope marked 'Private Practice' to the British Dietetic Association (see page 203).

Some NHS dietitians will also see patients privately, so try contacting your local hospital direct and speaking to someone in the Dietetic Department. Note that you will probably be asked to get a referral from your GP before your child can be seen. If you have private healthcare cover for your child, you may be able to claim the dietitian's fees back (check with your insurer).

As a parent, you can only try your best. Children will never be the little angels we want, so keep your expectations realistic and never give up. Improvements in eating habits can take a long time, sometimes years, but even small, slow changes are better than none at all. Be patient, keep striving to improve your child's diet and lifestyle and he will reap the rewards later on. We hope that following the advice in this book will help you to give your child the best start in life.

Useful addresses

Allergy UK
Deepdene House
30 Bellegrove Road
Welling
Kent DA16 3PY
Tel: 020 8303 8583
Website: www.allergyfoundation.com

Anaphylaxis Campaign
PO Box 275
Farnborough
Hampshire GU14 6SX
Tel: 01252 542029
Website: www.anaphylaxis.org.uk

British Dietetic Association
5th Floor, Charles House
148/9 Great Charles Street
Queensway
Birmingham B3 3HT
Tel: 0121 200 8080
Website: www.bda.uk.com

Food Allergy and Anaphylaxis
Website: www.foodallergy.org

National Childbirth Trust (NCT)
Alexandra House
Oldham Terrace
London W3 6NH
Breast-feeding helpline: 0870 444 8708
Website: www.nctpregnancyandbabycare.com

NHS Direct
Tel: 0845 4647
Website: www.nhsdirect.nhs.uk

Nutrition Society
10 Cambridge Court
210 Shepherd's Bush Road
London W6 7NJ
Website: www.nutsoc.org.uk

Vegan Society
Donald Watson House
7 Battle Road
St Leonards-on-Sea
East Sussex TN37 7AA
Tel: 01424 427393
Website: www.vegansociety.com

Further reading

Solve Your Child's Sleep Problems, Dr Richard Ferber (Dorling Kindersley, 1986)

Coping with a Picky Eater: A Guide for the Perplexed Parent, William G. Wilkoff (Prentice Hall & IBD, 1998)

Easy Peasy: Real Food for Kids Who Want to Cook, Mary Contini & Pru Irvine (Ebury Press, 1999)

The New Contented Little Baby Book, Gina Ford (Vermilion, 1999)

Food Allergies: Enjoying Life with a Severe Food Allergy, Tanya Wright (Class Publishing, 2001)

Kid's Food for Fitness, Anita Bean (A & C Black, 2002)

The Contented Little Baby Book of Weaning, Gina Ford (Vermilion, 2002)

First Foods Fast: How to Prepare Good, Simple Meals for Your Baby, Lara Boyd (Luath Press, 2003)

Index